THE
Chronicles of Destiny
FORTUNE CARDS

Josephine Ellershaw and Emily Ellershaw
Artwork by Claudia McKinney

4880 Lower Valley Road • Atglen, PA 19310

Image and model credits: Amber Ornelas, Beccy Dancer at LadyxBoleyn.deviantart.com, Devin Montiel, Dominic Arizona Bonuccelli, Elandria Broughton-Sheard, Gabriel Mantis, Gracefully Wicked Photography, Hannah Meadows, Ida M. W. Larsen - Mizzd-Stock, Johanna Chambers, Alexandra Bibby, Linda Kindt, Kirilee Lennerts, Lisa Baghepour, Rachel Ailin, Maria Amanda Schaub, Marisa Svalstedt, Michael Legge, Russell Sellers Photography, Teresa Yeh Photography.

Some images are from Shutterstock, Dreamstime, DeviantArt, DepositPhotos, Fotolia. www.deviantart.com/art/dramatic-clouds-217083699; www.deviantart.com/art/3d-Pirate-Ship-Png-Pack-5-373587061; www.deviantart.com/art/Mountain-Landscape-Stock-V1-406044107; http://darkrose42-stock.deviantart.com/art/Stormy-sea-55513661.

Copyright © 2014 by Josephine Ellershaw, Emily Ellershaw, & Claudia McKinney

Library of Congress Control Number: 2014942146

All rights reserved. No part of this work may be reproduced or used in any form or by any means—graphic, electronic, or mechanical, including photocopying or information storage and retrieval systems—without written permission from the publisher.

The scanning, uploading and distribution of this book or any part thereof via the Internet or via any other means without the permission of the publisher is illegal and punishable by law. Please purchase only authorized editions and do not participate in or encourage the electronic piracy of copyrighted materials.

"Schiffer," "Schiffer Publishing, Ltd. & Design," and the "Design of pen and inkwell" are registered trademarks of Schiffer Publishing, Ltd.

Designed by John P. Cheek
Type set in Prince Valiant/Book Antiqua

ISBN: 978-0-7643-4624-8
Printed in China

Schiffer Books are available at special discounts for bulk purchases for sales promotions or premiums. Special editions, including personalized covers, corporate imprints, and excerpts can be created in large quantities for special needs. For more information contact the publisher:

Published by Schiffer Publishing, Ltd.
4880 Lower Valley Road
Atglen, PA 19310
Phone: (610) 593-1777; Fax: (610) 593-2002
E-mail: Info@schifferbooks.com

For the largest selection of fine reference books on this and related subjects, please visit our website at
www.schifferbooks.com.
We are always looking for people to write books on new and related subjects. If you have an idea for a book, please contact us at
proposals@schifferbooks.com.

This book may be purchased from the publisher.
Please try your bookstore first.
You may write for a free catalog.

For You, Dear Seeker.

Epigraph

Many cultures believed the letters of their alphabets were far more than just symbols for communication, recording transactions, or recalling history. They believed letters were powerful magical symbols that could be used to cast spells and predict the future.

Christopher Vogler
The Writer's Journey

Acknowledgments

We would all like to give sincere thanks to Pete Schiffer, Dinah Roseberry, and the team at Schiffer Publishing, who have been an absolute pleasure to work with and so accommodating to our vision for this creative project.

Josie and Emily would especially like to thank Claudia McKinney for joining us on this adventure; her beautiful images brought the Kingdom and its magical characters to life, and without her this project would not have been possible.

From Josie...

Sincere thanks to friends and private students for their insight and enthusiasm as they worked with the deck during its creation, most particularly Judy Wolford, Deb Barrett, and Jennifer Lapidus. To my readers who encourage and inspire, and to my nearest and dearest for their steadfast support whilst I disappear to write.

From Emily...

To my husband, Dave, for his unwavering encouragement and support – a book deadline two weeks before our wedding certainly kept us busy; thank you for being my strength and keeping me sane.

From Claudia...

I would like to thank my family for always being so supportive, watching me spend crazy hours at my desk and never complaining. To my husband, Michael, who took good care of me as I worked to get things "just so."

I would also like to thank Emily and Josie for including me in this project and having the faith in me to bring their vision into pictures. It was my supreme honor and joy!

Contents

INTRODUCTION 8
HOW TO USE THIS SET 11
THE CHRONICLES OF DESTINY ~ PROLOGUE 13

Chapter 1 ~ The Enchanted Emporium 15
Chapter 2 ~ Guardian of the Books 17
Chapter 3 ~ The Hero 19
Chapter 4 ~ The Heroine 21
Chapter 5 ~ Dreams 23
Chapter 6 ~ The Call 25
Chapter 7 ~ Whispering Hall 27
Chapter 8 ~ The Elder 29
Chapter 9 ~ Accepting the Quest 31
Chapter 10 ~ The Adventure 33
Chapter 11 ~ Innocence 35
Chapter 12 ~ The Lightbearer 37
Chapter 13 ~ Time Flies 39
Chapter 14 ~ Distant Shores 41
Chapter 15 ~ The Lighthouse 43
Chapter 16 ~ Sinking Ship 45
Chapter 17 ~ Shore of Trials 47
Chapter 18 ~ Road to Nowhere 49
Chapter 19 ~ Pegasus 51
Chapter 20 ~ The Warlock 53
Chapter 21 ~ The Baroness 55
Chapter 22 ~ Masquerade 57
Chapter 23 ~ The Songbird 59
Chapter 24 ~ The Dragon 61
Chapter 25 ~ Downfall 63
Chapter 26 ~ Sorrow 65
Chapter 27 ~ Word on Wing 67
Chapter 28 ~ Forest Labyrinth 69
Chapter 29 ~ The Gatekeeper 71
Chapter 30 ~ Balance 73
Chapter 31 ~ The Dreamcatcher 75
Chapter 32 ~ Waterfall 77
Chapter 33 ~ The Fellowship 79
Chapter 34 ~ Interlude 81
Chapter 35 ~ Shooting Star 83
Chapter 36 ~ Kissed 85
Chapter 37 ~ Polaris 87
Chapter 38 ~ Weaver of Words 89
Chapter 39 ~ Resolve 91
Chapter 40 ~ Phoenix 93
Chapter 41 ~ Conflict 95
Chapter 42 ~ Victory 97
Chapter 43 ~ Book of Destiny 99
Chapter 44 ~ Ruler of the Realm 101
Chapter 45 ~ Knighthood 103
Chapter 46 ~ Treasure 105
Chapter 47 ~ Union 107

Chapter 48 ~ Bliss..........................109
Chapter 49 ~ Calendar 111
Chapter 50 ~ Alchemy....................113
Chapter 51 ~ The Butterfly Queen...........115
Chapter 52 ~ Castle........................117
Chapter 53 ~ Review 119
Chapter 54 ~ Mastery 121

THE SUPPORTING CAST 122
Supporting Cast 55 ~ Lady Spring.........125
Supporting Cast 56 ~ Lady Summer.......127
Supporting Cast 57 ~ Lady Autumn.......129
Supporting Cast 58 ~ Lady Winter.........131
Supporting Cast 59 ~ Hero II 133
Supporting Cast 60 ~ Heroine II 135

READING THE CARDS
    Let's Get Started! 137
    About Keywords.........................138
    Preparing to Read.........................139
    Asking Questions.........................140
    About Card Spreads.....................140
    The Art of Reading........................141
        Open Book Spread 143
        Summary Spread..........................144

    Alternate Realities Spread...............145
    Relationship Spread......................146
    Sequel Spread 147
    Story Spread..........................148
    Create Your Theme......................148
Story Spread Reading Technique ...149
    Example Story Spread With
    Theme Card 151
    Example Story Spread Without
    Theme Card 152
Indications for Time........................153
    Example to Calculate Time Period...155
Reading for Others..........................156
    Ethics and Responsible Reading.......156
Clearing the Cards 157
How Accurate are the Readings?....158

EPILOGUE 159
KEYWORDS AT A GLANCE..........160
BIBLIOGRAPHY..........................168
ABOUT THE AUTHORS 169
ABOUT THE ARTIST....................170

Introduction

Do you remember the first story you were ever told? Or perhaps your favorite book where the story wrapped itself around you as you became immersed within its world? Folklore, fables, myths, legends, and fairy tales woven with allegory: stories are as ingrained in our way of life today as they were for our ancestors.

Evidence of storytelling exists from ancient cultures and dates back many thousands of years in the form of cave paintings, followed by oral storytelling traditions, long before the written word. Stories served to chronicle events, instruct and educate, preserve traditions, promote moral values, and entertain, and they have continued ever since, in every culture across the world.

Over the centuries, alphabets and the written word emerged, recorded upon all manner of materials to gradually evolve into the form we now recognize as the book. The history of books is such a vast subject within itself that it would take an entire tome to cover the fascinating details, and an evolution that still continues with the advancement of technology. Yet the purpose that lies at its core remains unchanged.

References to prophecy using books can be found dating back to ancient Greece and Roman times, notably the Sibylline Books from around the 5th Century B.C., and Socrates was said to use the method of Sortes Homericae (selecting a random sentence from the work of Homer) whilst in prison. The term became known as Bibliomancy (originating from "biblio," meaning "books," and "mancy" for "divination") and was practiced across different cultures by consulting sacred texts. Oracles and seers have a rich history from antiquity and were consulted by leaders for important events and in times of crisis.

Having grown up surrounded by books and cards, our inspiration was drawn from these elements to create *The Chronicles of Destiny Fortune Cards*, which is centered on a book theme containing a story, and were specially created as a fortune-telling system to help provide insight and guidance. Divination with cards is also known as cartomancy, another ancient custom from centuries past that encompasses different traditions, including ordinary playing cards, Lenormand, Tarot, and Oracle cards.

In response to various queries raised by card readers from Josie's mail bag, we began creating a deck to try to help remove some of the challenges people were experiencing and provide a system that was straightforward to use, but spoke precisely and produced accurate results. Our journey began in 2011 and, over a two-year period, the deck was formulated and consulted regarding its own creation, advising, guiding, and being tested, to reach the right balance. The result is the work you now hold in your hands.

Emily has a passion for literature that extends to all things book related, and we particularly enjoy fiction from the fantasy and magical realism genres. This was an important factor regarding the type of images we wanted in order to portray the atmosphere and feeling of having literally stepped right into the world of the book. We needed an element of fantasy but not too far removed from our ordinary world and we felt that illustrations wouldn't have provided the sense of magical realism we required. Claudia's images resonated with the world we wished to create, so we were delighted when she agreed to join us. At times, one of our biggest challenges was making choices from her extensive portfolio.

Universal archetypes play a significant role in storytelling, as well as certain card decks. Despite our best-laid plans of portraying some from a different perspective, it was interesting how we unintentionally returned to certain symbolism, a quiet reminder of the constancy of their influence.

And so it began. All myths and adventures appear to spring from ordinary beginnings, chance happenings, or an innocent remark; ours began with a simple "what if?" that whisked us away into a different world, a realm we thought was of our making, but took its own direction. Myths and metaphors woven into everyday lives, the fabric of history spinning through time immemorial, where past, present, and future converge between the spaces.

The Enchanted Emporium and Guardian of the Books cards were a loving nod to our bookshops and libraries, those hallowed and coveted places cherished by book lovers, and the knowledgeable bookseller who opens your door into the magical world of a particular book. But the metaphor extends further, as you'll see by the time you reach the Mastery card.

When we opened the door to The Enchanted Emporium we thought we were creating the world, but the characters arrived on the scene and made their presence known. They danced in our dreams and manifested in our lives as they told their stories, and set us to work aligning their intent upon the page. We could spend too much time recounting strange and magical happenstance that occurred along the way, so perhaps it is enough to say that we lived the journey of the deck. We may write our stories but we live our adventures!

We hope you enjoy *The Chronicles of Destiny Fortune Cards* as much as we did creating it for you.

Josie & Emily

How to Use This Set

Once you enter "The Chronicles of Destiny," you will discover that each card is numbered as a chapter and the sequence corresponds with a continuing story in the book to help you remember the card meanings.

The next section of this guide is laid out to resemble an old-fashioned storybook; each chapter contains a color plate of the card image with a short excerpt from the story and the card definition with deeper explanation underneath. The main keywords to summarize the meaning are shown as "The Moral of the Story." The final section of the book covers the theory and practicalities of working with the cards.

We would recommend reading the next section of short chapters along with your cards first, as the story chronicles the journey in a sequence designed to help you become familiar with them.

Whosoever enters "The Chronicles of Destiny" takes the role of the Seeker, as the person seeking answers to their questions. The image of the Seeker varies throughout the deck to represent any who may consult it, the Everyman, and their role in the story is described using gender-neutral language. When you first enter the story, then *you* are the Seeker; if you read the cards for someone else, then *they* become the Seeker.

The cards have been numbered for easy reference, although we also use them as part of a system to denote timing, covered in the latter section of the book. As we read books right side up you'll notice that the card backs have an upright orientation. The balance of the deck has been carefully arranged so you don't need to read reversed cards, and should any appear upside down, just re-position them.

If you're already experienced in other cartomancy traditions, then we hope you will find the deck offers plenty of scope for you to explore, whether as an addition or in combination with other decks in your readings, or by applying your own favorite reading methods to the deck on its own. What follows is an explanation of the way we have worked with the cards and the basis on which they were designed.

We're sure you don't want to linger any longer in meeting the cards, so let's do that next. Enjoy your adventure and we'll meet you on the other side.

THE
Chronicles of Destiny

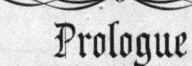

Prologue

   Welcome Seeker. Within you will find the threshold to another world, a doorway through the written word to guide you through your quest.
   A thin veil penned with golden ink is all that separates you from the answers you desire. Each card holds a story and the message you are seeking…

1. The Enchanted Emporium

The Moral of the Story is:

Learning and studying. Refining skills. Apprentice.
Curiosity provides the opportunity for discovery.
A path that leads to greater awareness.

Chapter 1
The Enchanted Emporium

On a certain street in every town, quietly nestled between unsuspecting buildings and invisible to the undiscerning eye, The Enchanted Emporium waits.

The shop senses a Seeker and shimmers into life, glowing in anticipation for the journey to be taken, the knowledge and secrets to be learnt. Golden lights flicker and dance within, enticing their curiosity to step inside and explore.

A solemn child emerges from the rows of ancient books.

"Name?" she enquires seriously.

With the Seeker's response, the charm she holds begins to sway, silvery chimes from tiny bells ring out into the hushed silence.

"Ah yes, we've been expecting you. Please follow me."

Card Definition

Your first encounter on the pursuit for answers begins with the apprentice. She studies under the mentorship of the Guardian of the Books, poring over pages to learn the secrets of myths and legends and how to apply the wisdom they provide.

The books and bird represent higher knowledge, whilst the candle flame and crystal indicate illumination. The child in white symbolizes openness to new ideas and the ability to absorb information.

When The Enchanted Emporium appears, it can show learning, and this may be in either a formal or informal environment. It could represent a course, such as through University or College, or your commitment to study and train to learn a new skill. It may also indicate that curiosity provides the opportunity for discovery.

Should this card appear with regard to questions concerning romance, it suggests staying open-minded to possibility and a path that may lead to greater awareness.

2. Guardian of the Books

The Moral of the Story is:

Occupation or workplace. Dedication to work.

Chapter 2
Guardian of the Books

The Guardian of the Books protects The Enchanted Emporium, home of ancient tomes and volumes with pages that whisper of adventure and faraway places. With golden ink, she carefully records long-forgotten tales, patiently gathering the knowledge to help the one she awaits.

She greets the Seeker with a knowing smile, sensing their growing wonder and curiosity. Hearing their unspoken thoughts, her fingers trace across the spines, searching for the book she knows to be theirs.

"It is said there is a magical kingdom where the answer to all life's mysteries can be found, that wonderful secrets will be revealed to the Seeker of pure heart and good intent, if they are but willing to make the journey."

"Can I go there?" the Seeker asks.

"Well, of course," she says, "let me show you the way."

She places the book into their waiting hands.

"Enter The Chronicles of Destiny; venture wisely and seek your fortune."

Card Definition

The Guardian of the Books has dedicated her life to helping seekers find the answers they desire. She holds the manuscript close to her heart, representing love and passion for her life work, the golden ink a symbol of value and higher wisdom.

When this card appears in a reading, it represents your occupation or workplace; the cards following would indicate the developing situation. For instance, should this card appear with The Call and The Adventure, it would show a new job offer, whereas with Knighthood, it could indicate a promotion.

The Guardian of the Books can act as a reminder that when we enjoy what we do, it's no longer considered work, but a vocation that fulfils us and provides a sense of purpose.

Should this card appear in questions concerning romance, there would always be a connection to work in some way.

5. The Hero

The Moral of the Story is:

For a man, this card represents himself in the reading.
For a woman, it represents her significant other (partner).

Chapter 3
The Hero

As the Seeker reads the story, they identify with the Hero, who must remain steadfast and strong when facing dragons or outwitting challengers on his journey. They associate with his struggles and triumphs as he embarks upon the adventure into the Kingdom to achieve his goals. The Hero resides within the Seeker as he represents their childhood aspirations for greatness, when life was regarded as an adventure and they believed everything was possible.

Card Definition

This card reminds the male seeker that he is the hero in his own life story. We all possess the capacity for greatness, yet our journey to attain it is often found through a series of challenges. The Hero embodies the energy of the male archetype and is not an interchangeable card, as the female equivalent is found in The Heroine.

When this card appears for a man it represents himself in the reading and its position in the spread will indicate to what extent he has, or will, exert his influence. The energies that will impact him are found in the meaning of the surrounding cards. Should this card appear in the final position, it shows that the result will in some way rely upon his actions or behavior.

If this card appears for a woman, it usually represents her partner. If she is single, this may be someone she is interested in or a potential new relationship; the surrounding cards would clarify.

4. The Heroine

The Moral of the Story is:

For a woman this card represents herself in the reading.
For a man it represents his significant other (partner).

Chapter 4
The Heroine

As the Seeker reads the story, they identify with the Heroine, who must remain steadfast and strong when facing dragons or outwitting challengers on her journey. They associate with her struggles and triumphs as she embarks upon the adventure into the Kingdom to achieve her goals. The Heroine resides within the Seeker as she represents their childhood aspirations for greatness, when life was regarded as an adventure and they believed everything was possible.

Card Definition

This card reminds the female seeker that she is the heroine in her own life story. We all possess the capacity for greatness, yet our journey to attain it is often found through a series of challenges. The Heroine embodies the energy of the female archetype and is not an interchangeable card, as the male equivalent is found in The Hero.

When this card appears for a woman, it represents herself in the reading and its position in the spread will indicate to what extent she has, or will, exert her influence. The energies that will impact her are found in the meaning of the surrounding cards. Should this card appear in the final position, it shows that the result will in some way rely upon her actions or behavior.

If this card appears for a man, it usually represents his partner. If he is single, this may be someone he is interested in or a potential new relationship; the surrounding cards would clarify.

5. Dreams

The Moral of the Story is:

Future plans, goals and dreams, but a need to take action to make them reality.
Aspirations and ambitions.
If surrounded by negative cards, it can show wishful thinking or being unrealistic.

Chapter 5
Dreams

The pages gently draw the Seeker in as they merge into this new reality, wrapping around them and absorbing them into the story. At the onset of sleep, lingering thoughts dance along the borderland of their dreams, spinning glimpses of unbound possibilities, far removed from the familiarity and routine of their ordinary world.

The cosmos waits with bated breath in the passing moments of time as dreams and decisions intertwine. Whispered hopes are whisked away by the wind and carried aloft. Ah, Seeker, do be careful what you wish for; someone somewhere is listening…

Card Definition

This card indicates something that captures your imagination, inspiring the mind to contemplate possibilities and daring you to dream. It represents your sleeping aspirations and ambitions being awakened.

Dreams is generally a positive card and shows that you are making or considering future plans; a goal may be in sight, but the necessary action will need to be taken in order to manifest it. The difference between dreams and goals are the steps taken to attain them, otherwise they remain no more than wishful thinking. With less favorable indications, it could show that the seeker is being unrealistic, but this needs to be taken in context with cards surrounding or following, depending upon the type of spread being used.

6. The Call

The Moral of the Story is:

An offer being made to you: a proposal or invitation that prompts a call to action.

Chapter 6
The Call

A breeze murmurs the Seeker's name with an urgency that cannot be ignored, beckoning them onwards. Following a glimmering light through the morning haze, they emerge into a forest clearing where the source is revealed as a radiant sword.

A maiden kneels before them, presenting the sword as she gazes upon the glowing aura and the essence of the lilting sound becomes hushed in the Seeker's presence.

"I deliver the sword that bears your name; you will need it to enter the Kingdom and take up your quest. You have questions only the Book of Destiny can answer, but will you take up the sword to recover it?"

Card Definition

According to ancient folklore, it was believed that bluebells were rung to call the Faery folk, with bluebell woods a place of their magical enchantments. In dream interpretation, they can also represent news coming. As an interesting note, in olden times, the sticky sap from bluebell bulbs was used as glue for binding books.

The Call represents an offer being made to you. This could be a job offer, a business proposal, an offer being made in a property sale, or a love invitation.

The context of what this offer represents would be found in the surrounding cards, but it will in some way indicate a proposal or invitation, and one that will prompt a call to action.

7. Whispering Hall

The Moral of the Story is:

Self-doubt. Not feeling good enough.
Lack of confidence. Insecurity.
Ignoring problems, denial.

Chapter 7
Whispering Hall

Initial anticipation starts to fade as a familiar voice creeps in from the corners of the Seeker's mind. Quietly it ventures in, sowing seeds of doubt and questioning their ability. Whispering reminders from the halls of time echo the memory of failures past, holding the Seeker captive in its sound. Motionless, they wait in the dark recess of their mind, lost in the wasteland of the Whispering Hall.

Card Definition

If the Seeker allows their fears to stop them, then they cannot move forward on their journey, thereby refusing to answer The Call. When we allow self-doubts to overwhelm us, it prevents us from making progress and we are left with the knowledge that insecurities prevented us from pursuing our ambitions.

The Whispering Hall represents the inner voices that hold you back, the niggling doubts that erode confidence and create uncertainty. Sometimes this may be due to fears created from a past experience.

It may also indicate turning your back on problems to avoid dealing with something, or that you are in denial and not wishing to face the reality of a situation.

The appearance of this card may suggest that you should not ignore problems, but consider the matter in a practical way and face the true nature of your fears in order to proceed.

The Moral of the Story is:

Elderly relatives or a person of mature years.
Taking advice from people with more life experience.
Maturity and wisdom.

Chapter 8
The Elder

The Elder meets the Seeker on their path and kindly notes their quandary.

"Everyone who came before you and each who will come after experiences doubt, but those who allow it to conquer them return empty-handed; we do not remember the heroes who did not act, they are swallowed unknown into history. Within you is a seed of greatness, but only when you recognize that strength will the seed begin to grow. Before you lies the Kingdom that holds the Book of Destiny, and much besides, but you must be ready to enter."

Card Definition

The Elder is cloaked with the web of life, the full moon an indication of her illuminated and reflected thought, gained through the fullness of time. The falling leaves allude to someone in the autumn of his or her life, or "golden years."

This card usually represents an elderly family member or a person of mature years. As a card of wisdom, it can suggest listening and taking advice from people with more life experience, our elders. An older person may feature in your life whose guidance could be important to you. Sometimes it can suggest taking a mature approach to the matter in question, but primarily we have found it normally indicates an older person.

9. Accepting the Quest

The Moral of the Story is:

Contracts, agreements, transactions.
Making a formal commitment.
Pledging your oath. Taking up the challenge.

Chapter 9
Accepting the Quest

The Seeker regards the journey ahead with renewed purpose and grasps the hilt of the sword with both hands. At their touch, an inscription begins to materialize along the blade and they raise it to their eyes, reciting the words as they appear.

"Committed by oath and forged by steel, I bind you to your quest."

The weight of the words settles in the Seeker's mind as the sword fits comfortably in their hands, perfectly balanced in their grip.

Card Definition

Before knights of old took up their swords they were required to make a solemn oath of honor to their leader and their cause, a practice followed across different cultures.

When this card appears in a reading, it represents agreements, binding contracts, or transactions being made. Whilst The Call symbolizes an offer of some description, Accepting the Quest is the agreement and formal commitment to it.

In certain circumstances, it may suggest rising to a challenge that has been laid before you, literally taking up the sword. However, primarily this is the card to indicate important contractual agreements. Depending upon the question and accompanying cards, the following provides some suggestions as to how this could translate: Guardian of the Books would be a job or vocation, with Castle a property contract, and Treasure a financial contract.

10. The Adventure

The Moral of the Story is:

All types of new beginnings, the start of something new, taking a new path in life.

Chapter 10
The Adventure

As the oath is declared, an entrance is revealed and the Seeker draws closer to peer beyond the opening. The land of the Kingdom rises from the clearing mist and the path stretches out far beyond, as yet unknown but soon to be discovered. Partially obscured by trees, the Seeker realizes they cannot see any further until they begin to travel down the pathway before them. Filled with hopeful expectation, yet uncertain as to what they will find, they finally cross the threshold into the new adventure.

Card Definition

The Seeker has one foot in each world, the known and the unknown, as they stand on the threshold of the new adventure. The opening represents a new opportunity, with the mist symbolizing what cannot yet be seen, and although the path may remain hazy, the light in the distance illuminates the way ahead. The ladder can suggest climbing or moving up whilst the telescope signifies looking ahead, so both can be representative of moving towards a goal.

When The Adventure appears in a reading it indicates a new beginning, a door being opened that leads to a new path in life, and usually something that's unfamiliar, unknown, or outside of your present experience. A positive and exciting card, The Adventure shows a new opportunity arriving in your life.

Surrounding cards will help to provide more information. For instance, with the Story Spread the preceding card would identify where the opportunity originates or what the new beginning is connected to, whilst the card following will show where the new path would lead.

11. Innocence

The Moral of the Story is:

Children or birth. Embracing life with a sense of wonder.
Keeping an open heart and mind.
Playfulness, joy, and innocence.

Chapter 11
Innocence

The Seeker is so focused upon the path ahead that they are caught by surprise when a small hand suddenly grips their own.

Their gaze is met by a wide-eyed child. "Where are you going?"

"I'm searching for my destiny."

"What's your destiny? What does it look like?"

"Well . . . I'm not really sure; that's why I'm here."

"But if you don't know what it looks like, then how can we find it?" Without waiting for the answer, the child skips back into the meadow, burying her head in flowers as she goes. Her laughter rings out as she waves for the Seeker to join her. "Come on," she cries, "my friend will know."

The Seeker contemplates the road they were traveling before stepping into the meadow to join the child.

Card Definition

Even though they don't know where they're going, the Seeker is fixed upon the path, but the child encourages them to follow and immerse themselves in the wild meadows of childhood, strewn with yellow flowers of cheerfulness, play, and discovery.

This card can be taken to represent a child in the reading. If accompanied by Lady Spring, it may indicate pregnancy, whilst with Lady Autumn could bring news of a birth.

Innocence also represents the nature of children, a gentle reminder to keep playfulness alive and those qualities sometimes lost through conditioning as we enter adulthood. The child embraces life with a sense of wonder and an endless stream of questions to feed their growing curiosity, yet often we may gain remarkable wisdom or profound insight from their imagination and open perspective.

12. The Lightbearer

The Moral of the Story is:

Someone showing kindness to you.
Gifts, generosity, and favors.

Chapter 12
The Lightbearer

She glides gracefully toward the Seeker on gossamer wings, surrounded by an iridescent light emanating from the object she carries. The sounds of the meadow fade, as even the insects and birds fall into silenced wonder at her presence. She beckons the Seeker forth as she proffers the bright object in her outstretched hands.

"A gift to help you on your quest."

The Seeker marvels at the magical light and at their touch a warm sensation floods through their being before it disappears.

"Where did it go?" they ask in surprise.

"Your destiny is in your heart," she says with a smile. "You just need to follow where it leads."

Card Definition

The Faery folk are often associated with bestowing gifts or favors, so The Lightbearer indicates a gift being given to you. The heart-shaped light represents the warm inner glow we experience when we're the recipient of someone's kindness of heart or generous spirit.

Gifts, generosity, and favors are all indicated with this card, so it is always associated with something pleasant that you're happy to receive. Alongside Treasure, it may represent a gift of money or a precious item but, as always, more information can be found in surrounding cards.

13. Time Flies

The Moral of the Story is:

Time flies.
Fast moving time frame,
things happening quickly.

Chapter 13
Time Flies

"You're late, you know."

The Seeker turns to the sound of the woman's voice, "I'm sorry?"

"Well, it's ticking you see...the clock." She points behind her. "Can you hear that?"

"I don't hear anything," the Seeker whispers.

"Exactly! That's the sound of time disappearing. The clock never stops ticking, always ticking..." She trails off dreamily, her gaze caught in the hypnotic sway of the pendulum, as the clock works toward the quarterly chime.

The woman stares at the Seeker as though coming from a trance. "But now you hear it, don't you?" she asks urgently. "The haunting rhythm of time marking passages of life disappearing."

The Seeker nods warily, uncertain of her changing moods.

"I waited too long, but how quickly time flies and now here I am, Keeper of the Clock." She sighs before suddenly brightening, "But it's not too late for you! Make haste for the harbor before the ship sails."

Card Definition

With her cloak of feathers the Keeper of the Clock reminds us that time flies, so this card can be helpful as a timing indicator.

When Time Flies appears in a reading, it shows a fast-moving timeframe, with events usually occurring within hours or days, or certainly within a few weeks at the most. However, this would also depend upon where it lands in the spread you are using. Should this card follow others, or appear as the outcome and final card, it can also show that once events do occur, they will happen at speed.

14. Distant Shores

The Moral of the Story is:

Foreign connections, people, or places.
International trade. A long journey.
Expanding your horizons to move outside
your comfort zone. Unfamiliar places.

Chapter 14
Distant Shores

White sails spread wide against a sky of promising blue to catch the breeze so that it may carry the ship to distant shores. The shouts of men onboard preparing the vessel merge with the cry of the gulls above, and everywhere there is movement, driven by a sense of purpose.

Laden with precious cargo, the ship sets sail, borne across an ocean to new and exotic lands. The Seeker gazes across the horizon, filled with excitement and anticipation for the long voyage and new discoveries that lie ahead.

Card Definition

Distant Shores represents a long journey with an international flavor. The ship crossing the ocean, map, and compass all symbolize faraway places with a foreign connection. Aside from holidays abroad, it can indicate international trade, as ships are often used to transport cargo. On a more literal level, it can sometimes suggest expanding your horizons outside of your comfort zone or to unfamiliar places.

Whatever cards appear alongside will also show the nature of the foreign connection. For instance, with the Castle it may suggest moving home, emigrating to another country, or a foreign residence, such as a holiday home. (One of our experiences with this combination represented a property owned by someone from overseas.) With Guardian of the Books, it can indicate international work or business. Alongside one of the cards representing a person, it may show someone from another country:

15. The Lighthouse

The Moral of the Story is:

Warning sign, a red flag.
Something demands your attention.
Danger. Proceed with caution.

Chapter 15
The Lighthouse

Rain comes as evening falls and a swirling mist seems to rise from the sea, engulfing the horizon in thick fog. The Seeker gazes out ahead, only to see the surrounding landscape fading, as though the rain were washing it away. Something flashes in the distance and the Seeker leans over the bow of the ship, straining to catch another glimpse. A light penetrates the gloom, blinking earnestly now at the Seeker. The rising wave lifts the ship and the haze momentarily clears before dense rain clouds burst open, but in that moment, the Seeker sees a column encircled by the sea. A lantern blazes atop the stone tower in warning – a lighthouse. The beam illuminates their surroundings and urgent cries go up from the sailors onboard.

In the distance, a heavy storm is brewing, although of such proportion the Seeker could never imagine.

Card Definition

Historically, the main purpose of a lighthouse was to warn of dangerous areas, although in modern times they are used more for guidance and navigation. This image shows a lighthouse standing on jagged rocks surrounded by a stormy sea and sky, so the beacon acts as a warning of danger. Think of this card as the red flag in the deck, trying to alert you to something that isn't right and demands your attention.

Always pay heed and proceed with caution when The Lighthouse appears, for even when more favorable cards surround it, the meaning does not alter. Look to see if a positive card follows, as this may show that you could safely navigate some stormy waters before achieving the positive result found in the final card.

16. Sinking Ship

The Moral of the Story is:

Loss of all kinds but particularly
financial loss or difficulty.
Failed plans.

Chapter 16
Sinking Ship

Towering waves crash down upon the ship as it rises and falls in the tempest, tossed insignificantly upon the vast, turbulent ocean. Caught in the grip of unseen fingers, the howling fury of the wind carries them perilously onwards toward the rocky reef.

The Seeker is cast adrift as the ship creaks and rolls, the shattering sound of the mast and rigging drowning out against the noise of the roaring sea. The raw brutality from the forces of nature conspires against the ship's fate, as it is finally claimed by the ocean and sinks to the depths of the watery void.

Card Definition

As the name suggests, the Sinking Ship is going down, so it represents loss and failed plans in relation to the question that has been asked, or as surrounding cards indicate. Ships were particularly used to carry cargo so this card would be the prime indication for financial loss of some kind.

The Seeker has been thrown from the vessel and separated from their material possessions in the process. As such, it can indicate temporary hardship or a period where financial difficulty is encountered; this could be as straightforward as an unexpected bill appearing at an inopportune time.

If this card appears in a future position, take care with financial dealings; avoid entering into a new financial commitment until the storm has passed.

17. Shore of Trials

The Moral of the Story is:

Challenging times. Trials and tribulations.
Difficulty, upheavals, stress,
(may show strained relationships).

Chapter 17
The Shore of Trials

Consciousness returns, slowly tugging at the Seeker's mind like the ebb and flow of the waves at their feet. With awareness comes the dull ache of heavy limbs, as though the weight of the ocean were still upon them. A burning sensation claws its way from their lungs, with every ragged breath grating at their throat until they feel raw. Fragments of hazy memory surface, a vague recollection of the struggle in the ocean before a dark void slipped across their senses, together with the gradual realization they are stranded, far from their destination and far away from home.

Card Definition

The Shore of Trials represents challenging times and so reflects various types of trials and tribulations. It can show difficulties being encountered, upheavals, stressful situations, or strained relationships. However, it will depend upon your question and the card's position in the spread being used, as it may just indicate a temporary situation.

Should this card appear in the final and outcome position to a question, then this result is advising of the challenges you will most likely face. It provides the warning that things won't be easy if you follow the particular course of action you have asked about. The Sequel Spread, or Alternate Realities Spread, can be helpful in this type of situation to explore other possibilities and find an alternative course of action.

18. Road to Nowhere

The Moral of the Story is:

Dead end or full stop.
Reconsider plans; a new route is needed.

Chapter 18
Road to Nowhere

The Seeker gazes out across the water; beyond the rocky shoreline they spy the dark line on the horizon that is the realm of their destination, seemingly unreachable now with the ocean between them and no vessel to carry them across. Night falls and soon the horizon is concealed by darkness; the path the Seeker intended to take is no more.

Card Definition

Road to Nowhere leads to a dead end. It's like encountering a broken bridge on your journey, requiring a new route to be taken in order to arrive at your planned destination.

Whilst Downfall acts as a definite "no," the Road to Nowhere suggests finding a different way around something, or taking a different route. It may not mean your goal is unreachable, but rather that you will need to find a different way to get there or reconsider the goal altogether.

Although you could consider this as one of the less favorable cards in the deck, as it doesn't provide the response you were hoping for, on the positive side, it can save you time and disappointment in the long run. The title of this card is quite literal, so concentrate your thoughts on a new path rather than expending all your efforts traveling down a road that will lead you nowhere. The Alternate Realities Spread can be useful to explore other options.

19. Pegasus

The Moral of the Story is:

Short journey. Flying visit.
Forward momentum, going places.
Speed, gets things moving. Transport.

Chapter 19
Pegasus

Lightning crashes down from the sky and, for a moment, the Seeker fears the storm has returned; another bolt strikes into the sea as a magnificent winged horse emerges from the waves. The creature kneels before the Seeker, offering his strength so the journey may continue. Once mounted, they set off at a gallop, hooves pounding the earth like thunder, and they take to the sky, leaving the trials faced at sea many leagues behind. The blur of barren landscape fades into leafy green, as Pegasus alights close to the shelter of a forest.

Card Definition

In Greek mythology, Pegasus has connections to the Muses, appears as the winged steed to heroes and Gods, and was later immortalized as a constellation of stars. Nowadays, the flying horse is often used as a symbol of speed and travel.

The Pegasus card represents a short journey or flying visit and the element of speed indicates destinations reached quickly, whereas longer journeys or foreign travel are shown by Distant Shores.

There is also an aspect of forward momentum with this card, accompanied by a sense of purpose and drive, so it may figuratively suggest you are "going places." Pegasus tends to speed things up and gets things moving. Primarily though it is the card of short and speedy journeys, travel, and quick visits.

20. The Warlock

The Moral of the Story is:

Delays and hold ups.
Obstacles. Sometimes theft.

Chapter 20
The Warlock

A phantom voice from the shadows cries out in a guttural language, bringing Pegasus and his rider to a standstill, transfixed by an unknown power. The Seeker eyes the challenger as he steps forward from the gloom, blocking their path with his sword aimed directly toward them. A further cryptic command summons a rope to his bidding, springing forward from his jacket to snake around the horse's head. The bridle tightens, causing Pegasus to rear and throw his rider heavily to the ground. The Warlock takes off with his valued prize, leaving the Seeker stunned and further delayed on the journey.

Card Definition

The Warlock card is an obstacle that blocks your path and often appears when there will be a delay and things are held up. Sometimes it can suggest theft, although from our experience, it more often indicates that delays could prove costly or result in out-of-pocket expenses.

As an example, this card appeared in a question concerning moving home and later proved accurate due to unexpected and unscheduled delays caused by the existing occupier. Whilst we couldn't place the aspect of theft at the time, the delays created unexpected expenses, including unreported repairs, which had not been anticipated.

The Warlock is the henchman to the antagonist of our tale, The Baroness (following next), so it is not unusual to find these two characters lurking around together in a spread!

21. The Baroness

The Moral of the Story is:

Underhandedness. Deceit. Hidden enemy.
False friends, or someone not working in your favor.
Manipulation. Jealously and gossip;
someone with a poisonous tongue.

Chapter 21
The Baroness

The forest is alive with whispers and word has already reached the Baroness about the stranger ambushed at the edge of her enchanted forest, a successful arrangement with the Warlock that works to their mutual benefit. All that remained was for the Baroness to sweep into the Seeker's life and play the "Good Samaritan," newfound friend, and charming hostess. She knew the plan would work perfectly, as it had so many times before, and she also knew the Seeker would have little option but to join her.

Card Definition

The beautiful Baroness appears against the background of the bleak twisted forest; the mask and fan represent the hidden side of her character and conceal her true intentions.

The Baroness represents a false friend, hidden enemy, or points to someone who is not working in your favor. There is always a component of deceit found with this card, which may be accompanied by manipulation, as someone tries to gain a selfish advantage at your expense. It can also suggest jealousy or gossip, often motivated by something you have that someone else wants. Although the image features a woman, this card is not limited to gender; however, it will always relate to a person, whereas Masquerade refers to an illusionary situation.

Despite outward appearances, it represents someone who is not to be trusted and does not have your best interests at heart. Pay attention to what is going on around you and don't be complacent or take things for granted, as someone is up to no good.

22. Masquerade

The Moral of the Story is:

Illusionary situations.
Everything may not be as it seems, be careful who you trust.
Confusion and clouded thinking. Secrecy.

Chapter 22
Masquerade

Ghostly hues reflect the haunting tones of twilight, as guests mingle in the shadows of the masquerade ball. Tables adorned with elaborate delicacies are set against a backdrop of lavish entertainment from performers in suspended gilded cages. Strains of music fill the ballroom and masked dancers sway in hypnotic rhythm, as a woman with gossamer wings begins to sing.

The Baroness offers the Seeker a goblet of wine before disappearing amongst guests and they drink deeply, without realizing the strength of the sweet tonic. Candles adorning the room throw elongated shadows, distorting forms into mystifying shapes, and the Seeker feels they have encountered a strange gathering of phantoms. Confusion begins to cloud their mind and the Seeker finally surrenders to the wine and weariness of the day, as the hushed conversation and muted laughter slips into the darkness of their dreams.

Card Definition

As the card of illusions, Masquerade warns that your perception of a situation may be different from the reality; something may not be all that it outwardly appears. Confusion or clouded thinking could also be masking the true nature of matters.

If you already have an uncomfortable feeling that something isn't quite right, but can't pinpoint why, then this card may help to validate your instincts, and surrounding cards may help establish the source. Don't take anything at face value at this time and look into matters more closely before making decisions. There can be aspects of secrecy suggested by this card.

23. The Songbird

The Moral of the Story is:

Restriction, feeling "caged in," stuck, or trapped. Dissatisfied with circumstances. Self-inflicted bad habits, addictions, unhealthy relationship.

Chapter 23
The Songbird

The Seeker wakes alone and, noting the lateness of the hour, they walk into the garden to clear their head. They are preoccupied by the beauty of the diamond-studded sky until a small sound attracts their attention. The Seeker is shocked to see the singer from the masquerade ball sitting inside a cage amongst the trees.

"Quickly," she whispers, "it isn't safe here." She gestures to other cages behind her, each with a forlorn-looking occupant. "The Baroness collects us because we have certain gifts, but she drains your magic to increase her powers. See how my wings fade? They were a Faery gift to help me before I was captured . . ."

The Seeker nods as they strain to listen.

"She'll treat you like royalty until a new soul arrives, and then you'll be imprisoned like us. You must escape; you don't want to be a songbird trapped and locked away, singing for your supper. Please get help and return for us."

Card Definition

The Songbird sings a beautiful song, but it has cost her freedom, and now she sings from the cage that confines her. This card represents feeling restricted, stuck, or trapped by a situation and feeling dissatisfied with circumstances. Self-inflicted bad habits can also come under this card, as can addictions, or an unhealthy relationship.

As the image suggests, whatever area of life may be under question, it could leave you feeling "caged in" and restricted. Check surrounding cards to determine the circumstances causing the problem and how it may be resolved. The ideal card to follow would be The Gatekeeper.

24. The Dragon

The Moral of the Story is:

Worries or anxiety.
Fears, real or imagined,
are preventing you from moving forward.

Chapter 24
The Dragon

The Seeker realizes they must flee from the Baroness or risk being held captive in her castle forever, never to recover the Book of Destiny or return home from the Kingdom. Panic engulfs their mind as they race out across the grounds, narrowly avoiding a wall of flame that springs up before them. As if plucked from nightmares, a dark shape rises through the dense smoke taking the tangible form of a fearsome Dragon preventing their escape.

Card Definition

The Dragon is an imaginary creature of myths and legends, usually depicted as a fearsome, fire-breathing monster that needs to be slain in order to attain a prize. The Dragon represents the mental monsters that create inner turmoil and invoke fears, but it also suggests that you need to overcome an anxiety in order to make progress.

Whilst the Whispering Hall indicates doubt through insecurity or denial, The Dragon represents worry and anxiety, a card of mental anguish. As the creature of nightmares that wake you at night, it's the demon that stalks in the realms of your mind. Your fears may be real or imagined, but they prevent you from moving forward in some way. Recognizing our mental monsters for what they are can sometimes be enough to slay our own Dragon.

If using the Story Spread, check the preceding card to find the source of the anxiety.

25. Downfall

The Moral of the Story is:

Defeat and resignation, feeling spent.
Efforts not realized. Letting go.

Chapter 25
Downfall

Clouds gather across a darkened sky as the Seeker reflects upon the course of events that led to their downfall. Staring into the precipice of defeat they feel a sense of resignation, the failure of efforts that have not been realized. All their plans have gone up in smoke, scattering a trail of ashes in place of their dreams.

Card Definition

There is a sense of resignation with this card, for not only does it indicate defeat, but also the disappointment we experience when efforts are not realized and plans do not materialize as we had hoped or intended.

At this point in our tale, the Seeker has already experienced significant challenges on their journey, indicating that considerable efforts may have already been made or invested into something, and so this card represents the low point on the path, resulting in feeling weary and beaten.

If Downfall appears, it suggests that dreams and plans have gone up in smoke and it is time to let them go. When you have thrown your efforts into something that doesn't work out, it's difficult not to slip into feelings of failure or despondency. Whilst it may seem that events have conspired against you, when you think you have hit the bottom, there's only one direction left to go, and that's up! Despite best efforts, not everything in life is meant to be and sometimes we need to let it go and start afresh in a new direction.

26. Sorrow

The Moral of the Story is:

Sadness. Sorrow and regret.
One-sided efforts, unrequited love.

Chapter 26
Sorrow

The Songbird's words sit uneasily on the Seeker's mind, as the recognition of truth weighs heavily on their heart, shattering any illusions they previously held. The Seeker feels foolish for their naivety and misplaced trust, easily taken advantage of in this strange land of unknown rules. A silent stream of tears marks the sadness of their regrets; a stained landscape of perfection blemished with betrayal and tears.

Card Definition

The Seeker's tears fall upon a beautiful bed of roses in a setting that might otherwise appear perfect.

Sorrow is a card of sadness and tears, the moment of realization that we have been let down. There may be regrets or self-remonstration for actions taken or not taken, the words spoken or unspoken, yet despite sadness and self-debate over previous actions, the truth remains unchanged.

In relationship readings, this card may appear if you've been let down or your illusions have been shattered. Unrequited love is often found with Sorrow, but it can represent any type of arrangement that turns out to be non-reciprocal or one-sided.

As the name suggests, in whatever setting this card appears, Sorrow indicates an element of sadness.

27. Word on Wing

The Moral of the Story is:

Messages and news coming in
through any form of communication.

Chapter 27
Word on Wing

The soft murmurings of thousands of leaves carry the secrets of the Tree Spirits, rippling through the forest and gathering pace until they reach far beyond the land of the Dark Kingdom.

The Baroness frequently changes the enchantments of the labyrinth to protect her position and prevent captives from leaving, so the Dryads act swiftly, making arrangements and preparing a route for the Seeker to escape. The bird takes flight, carrying their message to the Seeker in familiar words they will recognize and trust. "Your destiny is in your heart; follow it into the forest tonight and destiny will find you."

Card Definition

Word on Wing represents news and messages coming in. Doves are usually seen as a symbol of hope, so this is generally news of a positive nature, unless it is surrounded or followed by less favorable cards. If you are using the Story Spread, check to see which card precedes it to show what the news may be concerning, or from where it originates, then the card following for an indication of what the news brings or where it may lead.

The news or message can arrive through any form of communication, such as mail, telephone, text, or even by word-of-mouth.

28. Forest Labyrinth

The Moral of the Story is:

Making a choice.
Considering options,
a decision is required.

Chapter 28
Forest Labyrinth

As guests gather for another evening of revelry, the Seeker slips unnoticed into the cover of the enchanted forest that surrounds the castle. At each turn they are confronted by an intricate maze of shadowy pathways that disappear further into the dark canopy of muffled silence. With no time for hesitation, the Seeker must make a choice, realizing there is no other option unless they wish to remain and accept their fate. They grasp the note tightly and hope their heart leads them in the right direction, aware that others now rely upon them.

Card Definition

The Seeker swings the lamp behind them so the path ahead is not clearly lit, and they peer down various passageways that look the same.

This is often our dilemma when confronted by a choice, as we cannot see what lies further ahead or the outcome of the decision we need to make. There can also be a sense of urgency when a decision is required and these factors combined tend to create a quandary or fear in making the "right" choice. If you are faced with this type of situation, then try to consider that it's more beneficial to have options rather than a fait accompli, which may not be to your liking, or that there are no wrong choices really, just different consequences. In this regard, the Alternate Realities Spread (**page 145**) may also be useful to you in exploring the potential outcome of your options.

The Forest Labyrinth card indicates having options and making a choice.

29. The Gatekeeper

The Moral of the Story is:

Unlocks obstacles or secrets;
doors being opened for you.
A lucky escape.

Chapter 29
The Gatekeeper

Through the darkness, a flickering flame alerts the Seeker to a waif-like figure waiting in the distance. She gestures for them to follow her and leads them to a solid wall that borders the Dark Kingdom.

"I can show you a new path, a way out," she whispers. As she holds up a silver key, the stones behind her submit to her will, shifting and parting to reveal a keyhole-shaped opening.

"Keep traveling until you reach the clearing where another helper will be waiting. This path will lead you away from the clutches of the Baroness, but the Book of Destiny is closer than you think. Go and recover; you will return before the end."

Card Definition

The Gatekeeper is a fortunate card because it may unlock an obstacle or secret, open a door for you, or provide a lucky escape. Whatever the situation, imagine The Gatekeeper appearing to unlock the problem and let you through. It is particularly good to find this card in the outcome or final position because whatever you are facing, you will come out all right in the end.

However, the keyhole-shaped opening indicates that it provides an entrance or exit, but it never locks or closes anything, so it would still need to follow a less favorable card, rather than precede it. The context of how the meaning applies will depend upon the spread being used. As an easy example: if The Songbird followed, you may avoid one situation only to find yourself locked into another, whereas if The Gatekeeper followed The Songbird, it unlocks the restriction. The difference depends upon the ordering of the cards.

30. Balance

The Moral of the Story is:

Balancing different aspects of a situation or keeping a balance in life. Ability to retain balance. Mental and emotional stability found through balance.

Chapter 30
Balance

As daylight dawns, the Seeker reaches a track dividing the forest.
"I'm up here!" a voice calls out.
The Seeker adjusts their vision to see a girl in the sky, standing on piles of books.
"I'm trying to keep the balance and adjust when it shifts, but the Baroness has been getting stronger."
"But what if you lose your balance and fall?" asks the Seeker.
"Then it's over, the books will fall from the sky and the story ends...no more Kingdom."

Card Definition

Balance is the midway and central-numbered card of the deck, the pivotal point where the story could go either way (an interesting quirk, since we hadn't consciously planned for this card to fall in the central position!).

The blindfold heightens the girl's senses and awareness as she adjusts her weight to balance on the books, whilst the rabbit and mouse watch, balanced on hind legs. The stakes seem to be raised, as we realize the books upon which she stands are high in the air.

When this card appears in a reading, it can show that you are trying to find equilibrium with differing aspects of your life, such as home and work, for example. Mental and emotional stability are found through achieving balance, so it's something we are often striving to attain.

With Treasure it could represent financial balance, literally balancing the books. As a balancing act usually involves more than one entity, it can suggest more than one thing in play; for example, with Guardian of the Books, it could indicate that someone is balancing their time between two jobs.

31. The Dreamcatcher

The Moral of the Story is:

Protection from bad influences.
Ability to land on your feet.
Synchronicity at work behind the scenes.

Chapter 31
The Dreamcatcher

The Seeker follows the new path that leads deeper into the forest; dappled sunlight trickles through the leafy canopy, chasing away shadows that now lay behind. Ahead of them, a woman sits in a golden hoop, her fingers deftly repairing the silver strands of a delicate web.

As she notices the Seeker's presence, she speaks. "How intricate are the threads that weave the fabric of our lives. Moment by moment they pass one into another, deceptively innocent in their apparent disconnection, yet all held together but by one tiny thread."

She smiles at the Seeker's puzzled expression and motions them forward to join her, "You are safe from the Baroness here; her forest ensnares unsuspecting souls, but mine is enchanted to protect them. Take refuge and recover for all will be well."

Card Definition

The Dreamcatcher is a favorable card that provides protection from bad influences. Synchronicity is at work behind the scenes, so no matter what you are faced with, you have the ability to land on your feet and overcome difficulty.

The Dreamcatcher originated from Native American Indians and was used as a protective amulet, providing protection from bad dreams by capturing them in the web and only allowing good dreams to remain and slide down the feathers. Peacocks have the ability to eat poisonous plants without suffering ill effects and this is represented by the peacock feathers in the image.

Consider The Dreamcatcher as a protective amulet that will help you overcome challenges or adversity.

32. Waterfall

The Moral of the Story is:

Heath and well-being, vitality, healing.
Going with the flow and trusting the
process. Patience.

Chapter 32
Waterfall

Sunlight filters through the trees as the waterfall cascades into sparkling water, dancing downstream to the river's song. The Seeker eases into the cool depths until the water gently carries them, weightlessly floating in a pool of serenity, letting the water wash over their troubles as it soothes their soul. The weary traveler rests from the trials of their misadventure, revitalized by the healing properties of the waterfall as the river tumbles onwards on its journey to the sea.

Card Definition

Water is considered an essential and vital ingredient for life, so the Waterfall symbolizes health and vitality. Aside from improvement in health or general well being, the Waterfall card can also represent the healing of a rift or strained relationship.

This card may also act as a reminder to go with the flow in a particular situation, rather than trying to work against it. It marks a passive time rather than action, and allowing events or situations to unfold in their own time. Water may appear gentle and passive, but bodies of water also hold powerful undercurrents that are capable of exerting great force when unleashed. More progress can be attained when you ride with the current instead of pushing against it at the moment.

33. The Fellowship

The Moral of the Story is:

Friendship and loyalty, reliable and steadfast.
Helpful friends and allies lending support.
Teamwork.

Chapter 33
The Fellowship

A rustling in the bushes alerts the Seeker that they are no longer alone and they find they are surrounded as others materialize from the undergrowth. An archer keeps vigilant watch on the periphery of the group, poised ready to spring into action. The Seeker is startled by their presence, but they approach with a gesture of friendship.

A man moves forward from the group and approaches with a sword, "I believe this belongs to you; we found it washed up on the beach, but by the time we arrived, you had already gone."

The Seeker thanks him as they accept their sword, once again feeling its power thrum through their fingers. "But who are you?"

The others move closer to join the conversation. "We are seekers here the same as you; we have separate quests, but share a similar purpose and common enemy. Alone we may fail, but together we could find victory through the support of our fellowship."

Card Definition

The Fellowship card represents friends and people you can rely upon who are loyal and steadfast; the placement in the spread will indicate the part they will play. This is also the card of teamwork, pooling your diverse strengths and talents to achieve a common goal. It may represent one particular friend or a group of like-minded individuals.

This is normally a card of allies, unless surrounding cards suggest otherwise.

34. Interlude

The Moral of the Story is:

Pause, rest, pulling resources together.
Fact gathering. Taking time out.

Chapter 34
Interlude

Refreshments are offered to the Seeker as their new friends share supplies and make room for the newcomer. Once hunger is satisfied, the topic of strategy is raised, pooling resources and information gained so far.

They discover everyone has traveled from different lands as stories and experiences from their journeys are exchanged. The Seeker contributes their knowledge of the Baroness's domain, gained during their brief capture; amongst the Fellowship is the Songbird's partner who listens intently for news of his love. However, the exact location of the Dark Kingdom remains elusive due to the constantly shifting enchantments the Baroness surrounds it with, for protection.

The Fellowship disperses for the evening, but encourages the Seeker to rest and regain their strength. They lean upon their sword and feel the warmth of its energy surge through their being.

Card Definition

When Interlude appears, it suggests a time for rest in order to gather inner strength. In work or material matters, this could also show that physical resources need to be pulled together or consolidated at this time.

Whilst the Waterfall indicates healing, or going with the flow and allowing events to unfold, the Interlude card is a pause in activity to rest. In relationship readings this may indicate taking a step back, or time out, if things have been heated or strained. If Waterfall and Interlude appear together, side-by-side, it can suggest convalescence and recuperation.

35. Shooting Star

The Moral of the Story is:

Good omens. Good luck and good fortune.
Bright prospects. Persevere in your goal.
Believe in yourself.

Chapter 35
Shooting Star

Feeling a sense of relief and optimism through the camaraderie of kindred spirits who have welcomed them into their makeshift camp, the Seeker makes their way through painted caravans to find their sleeping quarters. Under the silent witness of the golden moon, a shooting star bursts into life, scattering silver trails as it falls from the sky. The Seeker catches a glimpse of its brief but radiant passage, feeling heartened that the omen bodes well for the future.

Card Definition

Shooting Star is a card of good omens and indicates bright prospects ahead. It encourages you to believe in yourself and to persevere with goals and dreams. Whilst The Dreamcatcher acts like a protective amulet, the Shooting Star is a card that foretells good fortune.

A shooting star is a meteoroid and, if it survives the impact with Earth's atmosphere, the resulting stone is a meteorite, much revered by ancient civilizations for their magical properties as a heavenly gift. Our fascination with the stars goes back thousands of years, so they often feature in legends, perhaps best known through Greek mythology.

In the starlit sky, a shooting star stands out against the rest, so, in the right circumstances, it may also indicate fame. As one of the most positive cards in the deck, it represents good luck and good fortune.

56. Kissed

The Moral of the Story is:

Love and romance. Falling in love. Deep affection and heart-felt emotions. Romantic love.

Chapter 36
Kissed

The Seeker is on the edge of sleep when they hear the first soft murmurs. Through half-closed lids, still heavy with fatigue, they see two of their new friends sitting close to the fire, their heads huddled together, hands clasped, and whispering softly in the firelight under the stars. She holds his hands tenderly and he gazes at him as though nothing were more precious.

The Seeker turns away as they embrace, and finds their dreams infused with the lovers' rosy glow.

Card Definition

Kissed is always a card of romantic love and in matters of the heart this is the one you would hope to see! It doesn't indicate love in any other context; as an example, if it appeared with Guardian of the Books, there will always be a connection between love and work in some way, perhaps someone met or known through work, rather than being interpreted as love of work.

The image shows a woman nestling dreamily in the water, surrounded by fish with air bubbles rising. The water and fish represent the depths of emotion, the colors for warmth and passion, and the bubbles for the light and airy feeling that falling in love brings, the romantic stirrings felt following a lover's kiss.

For matters of love and romance, Kissed is the card to look for, committed or permanent love is found with the Union card, but even better if they appear together! With The Adventure or Lady Spring it could show a new relationship.

37. Polaris

The Moral of the Story is:

Something important becoming known
to you that provides direction and guidance.
A moment of inspiration.

Chapter 37
Polaris

The Seeker shields their eyes from the shining vision before them.

"You know me well, as one of the brightest," she says. "See how all my brothers and sisters dance around me, but I am the constant in their nightly parade."

The beautiful lights swiftly disappear into the sky, eclipsed by the face of the Baroness, and the Seeker awakens from the dream with a start. Their mind is flooded, as thoughts fall together in a moment of inspiration. The Seeker hurries to wake the others as they realize they have important information that may help them, from their observations of Polaris and the night sky when they discovered the Songbird in her cage.

Card Definition

Polaris is also known as the North Star, or Pole Star, and is sometimes referred to as the fixed or guiding star. Late Antiquity mariners used celestial navigation to chart their course and the Pole Star sits over the North Pole, making it a reliable guide in an otherwise changing night sky.

When you draw the Polaris card, it represents a moment of inspiration when you see something clearly. A missing piece of information becoming known to you that connects the dots. Polaris provides direction and guidance, so a vital piece of information will become known. This may be from your subconscious or sleeping mind, which, once set to work on a problem, often provides the answer, or it may be from something you hear or are told.

Think of Polaris as an "Aha!" moment that suddenly helps you see everything clearly and stay alert to messages coming in at this time. The card preceding it may help to identify the source of this information or guidance.

38. Weaver of Words

The Moral of the Story is:

Small ideas with big potential,
ideas taking off and taking form.
The power of words, tact and diplomacy. Writers.

Chapter 38
Weaver of Words

Armed with new information, members of the Fellowship use the diversity of their skills to chart their course and forge a plan to invade the Dark Kingdom. Recognizing the strengths gained from magical helpers who have aided them on their journey, they seek out assistance from the Weaver of Words.

The Seekers wait, mesmerized by the golden cloud of letters that jostle and juggle as if to her will before she plucks them from the air, spinning the words like yarn from her pen, as she weaves the fabric of their destiny upon the page.

Card Definition

When we read great works by celebrated authors, we can be left in awe by the magic they have woven with their pens. They take an idea, then skillfully and creatively craft the words upon the written page into a work of art that holds us spellbound.

The Weaver of Words card shows small ideas with big potential, ideas taking off and taking form. Whilst the process may begin with a small idea, it is then the careful work you put into something that will ultimately transform it into a successful outcome.

This card may also remind you of the power of words, for just as the Weaver of Words plucks them from the golden cloud that surrounds her, it is how they are used and ordered that can either elevate or destroy, and so it may advise tact and diplomacy at this time.

For writers, this card may be representative of the craft.

39. Resolve

The Moral of the Story is:

Resolve. Determination. Taking action.
"Strike whilst the iron is hot."
Having the courage of your convictions.

Chapter 39
Resolve

Filled with resolve, the Seeker strikes their sword into the fire, as they prepare for the battle that lies ahead. United in their cause, the strength of the Fellowship will be tested against all that the Baroness and the Dark Kingdom can summon to fight them. The Seeker knows that everything they came for is now at stake, it is time for courage and determination and there is no turning back.

Card Definition

There is a familiar saying that iron doesn't become steel until it's been through the fire, and this card represents the moment when resolve and determination are called for.

The Resolve card indicates it is time to take action, to have the courage of your convictions, perhaps to stand up for yourself and the things you believe in that are important to you. Note the Seeker's stance and expression in the card as they strike their sword into the fire, the element of energy and action—we can see he means business and the time is now!

Road to Nowhere would suggest changing direction, Interlude would indicate a pause, Waterfall tells you to go with the flow and be patient, but the moment for determined action has arrived when you draw the Resolve card. A helpful proverb to remember this card would be, "Strike whilst the iron is hot."

40. Phoenix

The Moral of the Story is:

Rebirth, second chances, revival, reinvention, something resurrected.

Chapter 40
Phoenix

A lady in robes of fire emerges before the Seeker; the flames roll over her skin like waves, but she remains unharmed as the core of the heat. She bids the Seeker to hand her their sword, which she raises high above her head as the flames travel up her arms, flaring outwards like the wings of the mythical Phoenix, before surrounding the sword in their rejuvenating power. She returns the sword to the Seeker saying, "Infused with the magic of Phoenix fire and restored anew, the sword will protect you from the Dragon's fire."

The Seeker is ready to rise from the ashes of their defeat.

Card Definition

As the name would suggest, the Phoenix is the card of second chances, something being reborn or resurrected from the ashes.

In relationship readings, this card can represent the revival of feelings or the opportunity to renew a relationship from the past. Check the surrounding cards for an indication of where the past connection lies; this could be a person, place, project, or situation, but in whatever guise this card appears, there will be something resurrected from the past.

In some area of life, it could be that you have the proverbial "second bite of the cherry!" However, if less favorable cards are present, it could equally revive a past problem, so be sure to carefully check the placement and surrounding cards.

41. Conflict

The Moral of the Story is:

Conflicts. Arguments, quarrels, strife, and upheavals.

Chapter 41
Conflict

The friends storm the Dark Kingdom and battle ensues as opposing forces clash. The Seeker knows they must stop the Dragon before flames swallow the Kingdom and all will be lost to the Baroness. Focused on their strategy, the Fellowship pit their skills against the enemy, as the heat of battle surrounds and consumes them. The Seeker feels the strength of their sword, as the fire from the Phoenix and Dragon collides.

Card Definition

The Seeker is completely surrounded by fire in the battle, as the Phoenix fire from the sword collides with the opposing force of the Dragon's fire. An excess of fire causes things to burn, so think of clichés such as red-hot tempers, fighting fire with fire, crash and burn, etc. Conflict is the card of battles, arguments, strife, and upheaval.

In order to see where the problem originates, check the preceding cards. For instance: with family or property it would be Castle, with friends it would be The Fellowship, The Elder indicates older relatives, Guardian of the Books for work, Kissed for love, Hero/Heroine (or Union) a significant other, whilst Treasure may show arguments over money and possessions.

Once you can see the source of the conflict, then check which card follows, as this will reveal the outcome. If you can identify the problem in advance, then it may help you to defuse and avoid a potential confrontation. In some instances, going head-to-head over something may be unavoidable, such as if you were fighting a legal case or higher authorities (Ruler of the Realm), so surrounding cards may help to plan your strategy in advance.

42. Victory

The Moral of the Story is:

Victory. Triumph. Success. Achievement.
You will come up trumps.

Chapter 42
Victory

As the Dragon falls, the Baroness is defeated, breaking her spell and hold on the Kingdom. The light from the sword streams through the sky, banishing every trace of darkness that once clung to the land. With the Baroness defeated, the Fellowship are free to attain that which they sought without opposition. The Seeker advances triumphantly, the prize of their quest now within reach.

Card Definition

Together with the Fellowship, the Seeker has conquered the final challenge on their path and so, this card represents the culmination of their efforts on the quest. In film or fiction, this would be the climactic moment of the plot.

Victory is a card of triumph and success. The attainment of a goal and successful endeavors all come under the influence of this card. As one of the most positive in the deck Victory responds with a "yes," in answer to your question. Victory brings the prize, the reward of the triumphant moment, and satisfaction in accomplishment.

This card indicates achievements, both large and small, although as the story suggests, it most likely represents the successful conclusion or pinnacle of something worked toward over a period of time. In whatever context Victory appears, it shows that you will come up trumps!

43. Book of Destiny

The Moral of the Story is:

Destiny is created when you actively pursue it.
Whilst fate may present certain circumstances
destiny unfolds once you move towards it.
Action shapes destiny.

Chapter 43
Book of Destiny

The Seeker is surprised that the fabled book seems of quite ordinary and unremarkable appearance, with no elaborate cover to imply the magical secrets that it holds. They catch their breath when they find that the bookplate contains a simple inscription bearing their name and, as they delve into the pages, they find the story of their life, penned in the familiar hand of the Guardian of the Books. The chronicles of their great adventure unfurl upon the written page, and as the Seeker reads, they become enlightened to the mystery the Book of Destiny holds and the final words they find written there, "Destiny is created when you actively pursue it."

Card Definition

When you take meaningful action in the direction of your dreams, it sets off a chain of synchronistic events, sometimes considered as meaningful coincidences. As the Seeker's journey demonstrates, some doors open and others close, helpful allies mysteriously appear, whilst challengers test resolve, casting light and shadows on areas to strengthen or abandon.

There is a special connection between this card and Dreams, Weaver of Words, and Resolve, since their meanings contain the sequence of actions shaped by the Seeker and echo the secret found within the Book of Destiny. If these four cards all appear in a reading together, they are most auspicious, since they form the practical basis for achieving success through the combined effort of thought, desire, and taking action.

When the Book of Destiny card appears, it is the reminder that you write your own book of life. Whilst fate may present certain circumstances, destiny is created and shaped when you actively pursue it.

44. Ruler of the Realm

The Moral of the Story is:

Higher powers of authority, the law, officials, large institutions and structured organizations.

Chapter 44
Ruler of the Realm

The Fellowship is called for an audience with the Ruler of the Realm. Surrounded by royal courtiers, the king sits upon the throne, resplendent in his robes of office, as he listens to the details of events that led to the defeat of the Baroness and the Kingdom being restored. Silent anticipation fills the room as everyone waits for the king's decree.

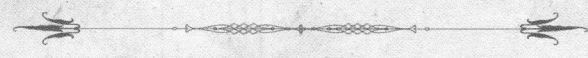

Card Definition

The Ruler of the Realm represents officialdom and higher authorities, not so much an individual as a governing body (council, trust, board, committee) of a structured system, such as the legal system or the law of the land, the church, government departments, large, structured organizations, or awarding institutions. It represents officials who make the rules that we must abide by or enforce those rules and have a higher influence over us. In some instances, it could represent your boss, but generally it indicates a governing body that makes or adheres to the rules.

Large corporations and organizations can come under this card, since they are run by a board of directors or for the benefit of shareholders; generally, when you see Ruler of the Realm, think big authority, not small.

45. Knighthood

The Moral of the Story is:

Awards and honors, promotion, recognition, approval from others. Someone holds you in high esteem or thinks highly of you.

Chapter 45
Knighthood

"Oyez, Oyez, Oyez! A proclamation by His Majesty the King hereby declares that Honors of Gallantry shall be conferred upon The Fellowship of Seekers in recognition for services rendered to the Kingdom . . ."

The public announcement from the town crier echoes around the four corners of the Kingdom, as the Seeker waits for their name to be called to accept their knighthood from the princess.

Card Definition

Knighthood represents awards and honors and indicates receiving recognition and approval from others for your efforts or achievements. This could be in the form of an educational award (look for The Enchanted Emporium close by) or, if preceded by Guardian of the Books, it could represent receiving a promotion or recognition at work.

This card shows that people hold you in high esteem or think highly of you, and this may be the interpretation if it appears in a relationship question.

As the atmosphere of the image shows, this does not necessarily need to take place in a grand public setting; it is the act of being honored and recognized for something you have achieved that is the most important sentiment, and this is the message the card conveys. Surrounding cards will help to clarify the context.

46. Treasure

The Moral of the Story is:

Money and material possessions,
usually improvement. Finance.
Someone or something precious to you;
valued and treasured.

Chapter 46
Treasure

The Fellowship take their leave from the royal court and are intrigued by the sealed box presented to each of them by the king to express his personal gratitude. Unable to contain their curiosity, the Seeker slips away from the crowds into the privacy of a wooded dell. They are surprised and delighted by the golden glimmer that escapes from the box, as it opens to reveal the treasures contained within.

Card Definition

Treasure is primarily the card for money and possessions, so this would be the card to provide information concerning finances.

Although all the cards rely upon the influence of those they are found with, the Treasure card, in particular, absorbs the energy of those closest to it. On its own or in the outcome position it is a favorable card, but those immediately before and after show from where it originates and where it leads. However, if this still remains unclear after you have laid out the full spread, you can take one more card from the top of the deck and place it over Treasure, and this is the final response at this time in revealing the source of the money.

In relationship readings, the meaning may be quite literal, showing someone precious to you or that you are valued and treasured (depending upon the position in the spread used). However, first and foremost, it is the card of finance and material rewards.

47. Union

The Moral of the Story is:

Commitment, marriage celebrations, permanency,
a settled and happy romantic relationship.

Chapter 47
Union

With the Baroness defeated, the Songbird has been freed from her cage and reunited with her betrothed, who had scoured the Kingdom for her. The Fellowship gathers to share and witness the loving union of their friends as they exchange their vows and commitment to one another. The ceremony provides a fitting tribute that marks the happy conclusion and culmination of their individual and collective quest.

Card Definition

Whilst Kissed is the card of love and romance, Union is the card of serious commitment, such as marriage and permanency. The Call and Union would indicate a proposal of marriage and engagement. If this card appeared with Ruler of the Realm it may show a wedding ceremony (the church, or being recognized in the eyes of the law).

For those who are already settled, it would normally represent a happy and contented relationship, although, as always, the following card would show what lies in the future of the relationship. For instance: Sorrow, Road to Nowhere, or Downfall would not bode well!

In a reading, the Union card always represents commitment or permanency in a romantic love relationship; for other types of commitment, such as business, work, or finance, you would look for Accepting the Quest.

48. Bliss

The Moral of the Story is:

Happiness and contentment.
Celebrations, a time of joy.

Chapter 48
Bliss

Bells ring out across the Kingdom, heralding a time for celebration and the subjects congregate to rejoice the return of peacetime after living in fear of the Baroness's dark powers. The Fellowship has much to celebrate, with the wedding of their friends, the attainment of their boons, and the honors bestowed upon them. Food and wine flow freely as music and laughter fill the air, and the Seeker joins the dance as happiness sings in their heart.

Card Definition

Bliss is the card of happiness and contentment and one of the most positive in the deck. The Seeker dances as rainbow colors permeate their being, reflecting the colors of the chakras in a state of perfect harmony.

This card can also indicate celebrations of all descriptions and surrounding cards should help to clarify circumstances, (e.g., marriage, birth, new home, new job, etc.). In whatever situation the Bliss card appears, it adds great joy and is further enhanced should Lady Summer or Lady Autumn also appear. It provides a perfect response should it appear as the outcome card in one of the positional spreads; with the Story Spread, look to the preceding card to find the source of the happiness that will be experienced.

49. Calendar

The Moral of the Story is:

Slow timeframe, months or years.
Slow movement but steady progress and lasting.
Delay or longevity, depending on placement.

Chapter 49
Calendar

Festivities continue long into the night as bonfires and beacons light the length of the realm. The Seeker sits back to catch their breath and watches the fireworks cascade through the skies. As the lights flare into life, they momentarily glimpse the image of a lady stood against the backdrop of a mystical calendar and their eyes meet briefly before her serene gaze turns back to the heavens. The Seeker understands her silent message as their thoughts return to the Keeper of the Clock. Seasons have passed and time has moved on, but the Seeker never noticed the passages of time disappearing.

Card Definition

The Calendar is yet another card that helps to provide an idea of time, and shows a slow-moving timeframe of some months, in contrast to Time Flies, which suggests hours or days. As always, the placement of the card in the spread will define the context.

For example, in the Story Spread, if the Calendar precedes another card, then patience may be required as it delays what it brings by quite some time, whereas when following another card, it may suggest slower movement, but steady progress and longevity. This makes a considerable difference if you imagine a question concerning money, for instance: Calendar, Treasure — as against Treasure, Calendar. Or a marriage question with Calendar, Union — rather than Union, Calendar.

Placement is everything with this card, so if you're waiting for something then the response could either be quite frustrating or extremely satisfying!

50. Alchemy

The Moral of the Story is:

Something ordinary has the potential to turn into something extraordinary. You only get out of something what you put into it, but you have the ingredients to create something special.

Chapter 50
Alchemy

The Seeker feels troubled by the implications of the calendar as they realize how much time has been spent pursuing their quest, with little thought about afterward. As they move away from the crowd to find refreshments, they are aware of their reluctance to return after the excitement of the Kingdom.

The lady seated beside them interrupts their thoughts, "Let me mix you something special."

From experience, the Seeker recognizes her as a magical helper and confides in her, "I shall miss it here; it's so different from where I came from."

"What makes you think you can't return, or that this world is truly much different from your own?"

The Seeker contemplates her words while she carefully measures and blends various elements, until a burst of color escapes from the ordinary cup as it turns to gold.

"You only get out of something what you put into it." She smiles as she hands the cup to the Seeker. "But you have all the ingredients for a magical life."

Card Definition

When Alchemy appears, it shows that something you may consider ordinary has the potential to become something special. This card adds a touch of magic to those in closest proximity, so if you're using the Story Spread, pay particular attention to the cards that fall before and after it.

The Alchemy card carries the reminder that you'll only get out of something what you put into it, but you already have the necessary ingredients to create something extraordinary.

51. The Butterfly Queen

The Moral of the Story is:

Catalyst for change;
brings a major transition and transformation.
Metamorphosis. The winds of change.

Chapter 51
The Butterfly Queen

She skims across the sky in a swirling mist of vibrant color, borne upon clouds of butterflies.
"Come," she cries, "the time is near."
"But where are we going?" The Seeker feels themselves being lifted into the air, gently gathered into the fluttering throng, as they become part of the dazzling kaleidoscope traveling through the skies.
"To ride the changing wind." She laughs at the Seeker's apprehensive expression. "Don't be afraid, there's so much more to follow."

Card Definition

When The Butterfly Queen appears it represents a catalyst for change. A major transition is about to take place and some area of life will undergo transformation.

The butterfly experiences four stages of metamorphosis in its life cycle: egg, caterpillar, chrysalis, and finally, a brief spell as a butterfly. The butterfly does not resist; it just becomes, as part of a natural process of growth, yet each stage is profoundly different from the last. With our longer life span, changing circumstances are inevitable, yet something we often strongly resist, perhaps because it is unfamiliar territory. Some of our happiest life experiences will fall into the category of major change too, so there is no need to view this card unfavorably. The Earth slowly spins in the corner of the image, referencing the continuum of life and ever-forward movement.

When The Butterfly Queen appears, it is time to spread your wings and ride the winds of change to where they may lead. Surrounding cards will identify the nature or circumstances of the changes but it's not unusual to find The Adventure close by.

52. Castle

The Moral of the Story is:

Your home is your castle!
Home and family. Property. Stability.

Chapter 52
Castle

"Our home is like a warm, safe harbor, the place where we carry our hopes and dreams to their rightful destiny, to share and rejoice in the treasure we carry, and our haven when the storms of life are high. How the heart lifts at the sight of those shores, safe in the knowledge we have found our way home."
The Butterfly Queen bids the Seeker farewell as she delivers them back to the safety of their home.

Card Definition

In 1628, a common law was introduced in England by Sir Edward Coke, "For a man's house is his castle, *et domus sua cuique est tutissimum refugium* [and each man's home is his safest refuge];"[1] a phrase still widely used and quoted today.

The Castle card represents home and hearth, the place you call home and the family you live with. Most of us regard our home as our haven and a place of stability, where we can shut the door on the outside world and relax within our own private space.

If you're looking to move home or buy/sell a home (tenancy or ownership), you would normally be looking for cards, such as The Call (the offer), Accepting the Quest (contractual agreement), Treasure (money and costs), and The Adventure (indicating something new). The Ruler of the Realm may indicate officials involved, whilst The Butterfly Queen shows major change, and Distant Shores suggests a foreign connection. Not all these cards need to be present but they provide examples as to how they might be relevant, depending upon circumstances.

[1] Coke, Edward. The Third Part of the Institutes of the Laws of England, (1628); ch. 73, p. 162, quoted in Angela Partington, ed. *Oxford Dictionary of Quotations*. Oxford, England: Oxford University Press, 1993, p 209.

53. Review

The Moral of the Story is:

Reviewing, taking stock,
answers lie in the past and past actions,
reflection. Past experience. Memories.

Chapter 53
Review

Back in the familiarity of their home, the Seeker reflects upon The Chronicles of Destiny and the incredible journey experienced so far. Their encounters with allies and challengers, dragons and royalty, disaster and triumph, are all the magical ingredients for adventure. They look back upon the advice received from the magical helpers, feeling they must have missed something important from their messages of wisdom. The Seeker carefully retraces their steps and finally stops to ponder the Alchemist's words. "What makes you think you can't come back?" The Seeker realizes there is one person who could provide them with the answer.

Card Definition

Review is the card of looking back and taking stock, so it can indicate that an answer you're looking for lies in the past. This card provides the message of reflection and reviewing what has gone before, as there is something valuable that can be learnt from past actions or experiences. You may need to retrace your steps, as there could be an important detail you have missed.

If something from the past were being revived in some way, then it would not be unusual to find the Phoenix close by, although if one of the less favorable cards follows, then you may be advised to let something from the past go.

54. Mastery

The Moral of the Story is:

Mastery. Integrating what you have learnt by applying skills and talents. Graduation.

Chapter 54
Mastery

The Seeker returns with the book to The Enchanted Emporium, eager to share their story, express their gratitude, and discover the last missing piece of their puzzle, but the bookshop is strangely silent. They venture into the back room where their wondrous encounter first took place, only to find an envelope bearing their name containing a brief cryptic note and a large golden key.

"For you, dear Seeker . . ."

Suddenly the shop bursts into life, golden lights flicker and a gentle whispering begins. They notice the pages surrounding them are numerically ordered into chapters, each bearing the names of stages from their journey. At their touch, they shuffle into a different order, shimmering with expectation to share their secrets in the new adventure that is about to begin.

In the background, a familiar bell rings out and the new Guardian of the Books instinctively understands what the seeker will need, as they prepare to pass on the wisdom from "The Chronicles of Destiny."

Card Definition

The Seeker has returned and, due to their knowledge and experience, they pick up the mantle from the Guardian of the Books to help others. It is time to make use of what they have learnt from their journey in the Kingdom, by applying the skills and talents they now possess into their ordinary world.

This then, is the message the Mastery card provides, it informs you that you have the abilities that are required to perform a certain task or deal with a particular situation.

Graduation in some form would also be relevant with this card, whether in an educational, formal, or experiential sense.

Supporting Cast

There are a few cards that play a background role as supporting characters, so they are not individually numbered as chapters in our story, although this does not diminish their relevance to us as they still perform an important function.

Each of the season cards provides two functions, first of all they contain a designated and distinct meaning, and secondly they can be used to denote timing.

55. Lady Spring

Keywords:

Green shoots and growth, new life, fertility (possible pregnancy with Innocence).
A new cycle beginning. Renewal.
Timing card, Northern Hemisphere: March, April, May. (Adjust for Southern Hemisphere.)

Supporting Cast ~ 55
Lady Spring

Lady Spring calls the earth forth to awaken from winter's dream, heralding a time of renewal as she breathes new life into the seeds that have slumbered all winter long. A new cycle of life commences as nature responds with green shoots, gradually painting the landscape in cheerful color, and creatures begin courtship rituals.

This card is associated with growth and the fragile start of new life, so all types of new beginnings are indicated. Should this card appear with Innocence, it may suggest fertility, conception, and pregnancy.

If the Phoenix card were present, it would strengthen the meaning of resurrection and renewal by association, as Lady Spring can sometimes show renewal and literally breathes new life into something. However, the main interpretation represents new beginnings.

We cover more detail for the timing systems on page 153, but for the Northern Hemisphere, Lady Spring covers the three-month period beginning from the 1st of March through to the 31st of May.

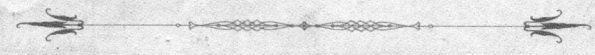

56. Lady Summer

Keywords:

Blossoming, in its prime, cause for celebrations, hive of activity.
Timing card, Northern Hemisphere: June, July, August.
(Adjust for Southern Hemisphere.)

Supporting Cast ~ 56
Lady Summer

Lady Summer's skirts are filled with flowers trailed across the land, and the evening air is perfumed from garlands woven in her hair. Nature unfolds to bask in the sunlight, encouraging creatures into a hive of activity, as growing crops are nurtured in readiness for the autumn harvest.

Summer brings the warmest days and longest daylight hours as the Sun reaches its peak and the earth blooms and blossoms in response. In ancient times, people celebrated the passages of the seasons as their existence was more reliant upon the natural rhythms and cycles of the land, particularly the Sun for its life-giving properties of light and warmth, so the summer solstice, or Midsummer, marked a time of great festivities. June was named in honor of Juno, Roman goddess of women and marriage, and still remains the most popular month of the year for weddings.

When this card appears, it represents something blossoming and in its prime, reaching a pinnacle. Lady Summer brings cheerfulness and celebrations, and the reminder to make hay whilst the sun shines. Together with the Union card, it would strengthen the association of a wedding.

For the Northern Hemisphere, this card covers the three-month period from the 1st of June to the 31st of August when used as part of the timing system.

57. Lady Autumn

Keywords:

Abundance, harvest, fruitful endeavors, collecting rewards, matters bearing fruit. With Innocence may represent birth.
Timing card, Northern Hemisphere: September, October, November. (Adjust for Southern Hemisphere.)

Supporting Cast ~ 57
Lady Autumn

Lady Autumn paints the scenery with golden hues; her crown bears the fruit of the season's bounty as the earth gives up her gifts, marking the time to gather in the harvest. Nature provides the glorious finale with a curtain of rich color before the leaves fall, in a final flourish and fitting swan song to the season.

The autumn equinox, when day and night are in equal measure, traditionally represented the harvest home, a time to give thanks for the earth's harvest, collected and stored, ready for the long winter ahead. Daylight hours shorten as the Earth continues the annual precession, and creatures take this last opportunity to increase stores or prepare for hibernation, whilst others migrate to warmer climes.

This card indicates the harvest, abundance, fruitful endeavors, collecting rewards, and matters bearing fruit, so the influence it holds is a good sign in any situation and the message of abundance provides an additional boost. Should Lady Autumn appear together with Innocence then it may represent a birth.

For the Northern Hemisphere, this card covers the three-month period from the 1st of September to the 30th of November when used as part of the timing system.

58. Lady Winter

Keywords:

Frozen. Patience required, matters developing although they can't be seen.
Quiet and solitude, dormant period, withdrawal, feeling isolated, an indifferent heart.
Timing card for Northern Hemisphere: December, January, February.
(Adjust for Southern Hemisphere.)

Supporting Cast ~ 58
Lady Winter

With sleeping butterflies tangled in her hair, Lady Winter makes her entrance, decorating the landscape with frosted fingers. She dims the Sun's lantern in the sky and, with a goodnight kiss, drops her white cloak across the land as it descends into muffled slumber. The blanket of snow provides insulation, as deep in the earth activity continues unseen.

The Earth's axis tilts away from the Sun, bringing the shortest daylight hours and coldest temperatures of the year. The Sun sits low in the sky and hibernating creatures withdraw until spring reappears.

Lady Winter freezes things, so this card indicates a dormant period when patience is required; matters may be developing under the surface even though they cannot be seen at this time. It suggests quiet and solitude, withdrawal, or feeling isolated. In relationship readings, it can reveal an indifferent or frozen heart.

Note the difference here between Lady Winter and the Calendar; one freezes something, whilst the other may delay them, but this also implies slow and steady progress. They are both slow-moving cards, but the impact will be experienced differently.

For the Northern Hemisphere, this card covers the three-month period from the 1st of December through to the last day of February when used as part of the timing system.

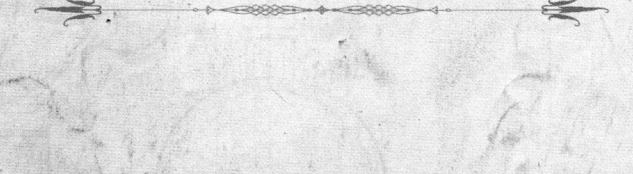

59. Hero

Keywords:

Can be used as an alternative card to switch with Heroine for same sex reading, or an extra card to include where another man may feature in a question. A mystery man, "tall, dark stranger," another potential love interest or rival.

Supporting Cast ~ 59
Hero II

Hero II is an alternative card that can be used in a number of different ways, depending upon your circumstances or requirements from the deck. Firstly, you can use this card to replace The Heroine if the reading is for a gay male, so this card would be representative of his partner, or a potential partner.

If you have a question or personal situation that particularly involves another man, outside of your partner, you could include this card to represent the named person. For example: your boss, an additional love choice where a choice of two men may be relevant, or a love rival.

As an additional character, the Hero II is neutral, allowing you to project your intention as to whom you wish the card to represent. This can be very helpful for readings where additional people are involved or may play an important role in answer to your question, but you need to decide whom they represent at the outset to ensure you're not left guessing who is who.

If you chose to do so, you could simply leave the card in the deck as a mystery man, or a "tall dark stranger!" Although as a card of neutral meaning, there is nothing further you will be able to disclose about him, other than as surrounding cards may reveal.

There are two neutral cards provided, one male and one female (following), so you can add them as designated people if they are relevant to your situation and they can be most helpful in that regard.

Of course, you may just prefer the card's appearance and decide to switch it with the other Hero card, and that's okay, too!

60. Heroine II

Keywords:

Can be used as an alternative card to switch with Hero for same sex reading, or an extra card to include where another woman may feature in a question. A mystery woman, "beautiful stranger," another potential love interest or rival.

Supporting Cast ~ 60
Heroine II

Heroine II is the female version of Hero II; it is an alternative card that can be used in a number of different ways depending upon your circumstances.

Firstly, you can use this card to replace The Hero if the reading is for a gay female, so this card would be representative of her partner, or a potential partner.

If you have a question or personal situation that particularly involves another woman, outside of your partner, you could include this card to represent the named person. For example: your boss, an additional love choice where a choice of two women may be relevant, or a love rival.

As an additional character, the Heroine II is neutral, allowing you to project your intention onto it as to whom you wish the card to represent. This can be very helpful for readings where additional people are involved or may play an important role in answer to your question, but you need to decide whom they represent at the outset to ensure you're not left guessing who is who.

If you chose to do so you could simply leave the card in the deck as a mystery woman, or "beautiful stranger!" Although as a neutral card, there is nothing further you will be able to disclose about her, other than as surrounding cards may reveal. There are two neutral cards provided, one male (covered previously,) and one female, so you can add them as designated people if they are relevant to your situation and they can be most helpful in that regard.

Of course, you may just prefer the card's appearance and decide to switch it with the other Heroine, and that's okay too!

The Hero II and Heroine II cards can provide additional flexibility into your readings, as you require.

Reading the Cards

Let's get Started!

There are some old wives' tales connected to cartomancy, such as needing to be gifted the cards, which you don't, or very precise methods for shuffling, cutting, storage, etc. For the main part, there are no absolutes; readers use varying techniques, so it is really just a matter of personal preference and consistency with your chosen method. The relationship you build with your cards is very much a personal one and the way you choose to work with them tends to reflect your own beliefs.

In the explanations that follow we have provided the way that we like to work with the cards, but feel free to explore until you find what you feel happiest with. Over time, you'll find a technique that works best for you as you become familiar with your deck.

Some readers don't like anyone else to handle their cards and they shuffle for the seeker, or spread the cards in a fan for the seeker to choose the cards for the spread. Other readers like the seeker to shuffle, so their energy makes a personal connection to influence the cards that appear. Some cut in a specific way and others choose not to cut at all, working straight from the top of the deck. As you can see, there are many variables!

We'd recommend spending some time "grounding" the cards by shuffling and cutting, as they can be slippery when brand new or stick together in clumps, but after a little while, they settle down. We prefer not to use casino-style shuffling or riffling though, as it may damage the cards. A ritual we personally like and follow is to sleep with a new deck under our pillow at least once. If you decide to do the same, then place them in a small cloth bag or tie them securely in a piece of fabric, so they don't get damaged or lost.

When not in use, you can store the cards back in their box or a drawstring bag, which helps to keep them safe from damage and ensure none go astray.

About Keywords

The Moral of the Story is: everything becomes easier once you know the keywords for the cards. Consider the keywords like foundations, because everything else builds on top and around them from there.

This book is laid out in such a way to help easily locate the chapter you need for the card meaning, or the "cheat sheets" on page 160 provide the keywords at a glance. However, once you reach the stage where you don't need to interrupt your reading by checking the book, you'll find everything flows together more easily.

The keywords act as a summary of the full meaning and help prompt your memory for instant recall. The fictional story that accompanies each card sequentially links them to make it simpler to remember what they represent. When you've followed this through, you could try putting the book down and go through the cards to recall the keywords.

Once you feel fairly confident, shuffle the deck and mix up the order. Allow yourself some time to take in the image before referring back to the book; you may be pleasantly surprised how your subconscious mind works to your benefit, digging deep into your memory to recover the information it knows to be stored there. The subconscious mind is like your own highly organized personal assistant, it knows just where to find everything when you set the task and give it a little time to respond.

You may find that you react differently to the meanings we've assigned to each card, or have another interpretation you prefer, and this is fine too, as the cards will respond to the intention you focus upon them. However, if you decide to completely alter any of the meanings, just check to see if it removes anything you might otherwise need from the deck, as it was structured for balance when it was created. The only other caveat we would raise is to be careful not to laden a card with too many different meanings, otherwise it could be difficult to decide which interpretation to use when it appears and your readings could become vague. The interpretations provided are clearly defined for this reason.

Preparing to Read

Once your cards are thoroughly shuffled and mixed, you're ready to begin reading! We like to use a dark cloth to place on the table, as it provides a clean surface to protect the cards and a plain background for the images to stand out against. As you learn the card meanings and become familiar with your deck, you'll find that your subconscious automatically connects with the images, so a plain cloth can help to prevent being distracted by other patterns.

Consult the cards when you're feeling calm and grounded. If you're upset about something, it would be better to leave the reading until you're feeling more centered, otherwise they could reflect your agitated state.

As you hold your cards, you may like to use an affirmation of silent intention to begin the reading process. It's like an opening ritual, signaling that you're ready to connect and tap into the mysterious flow of synchronicity that constantly weaves around us. Inwardly we recite something along the lines of:

> I ask for assistance to help me provide clear guidance in this reading. Thank you.

Then shuffle the cards whilst focusing upon your question. Try not to rush this process, as it's one of the most important ways to determine which cards will be drawn. When you feel ready, stop and cut the cards into three stacks, then place them back into one stack by picking them up in the order you dropped them, stack one on top of two on top of three.

Asking Questions

When addressing a question, try to make it clear, focus on one specific issue, and ask in the positive. As an example, if you were worried about your job because your company was making people redundant, it would be better to ask something along the lines of, "What is the future of my employment with (name of company)?" If you ask if you're going to lose your job, it can be confusing to know which way to read the cards' response.

By making your question unambiguous you should receive a defined response that you can more easily understand. Also, try to ensure that your question isn't actually a string of questions rolled into one.

For instance, a few examples for phrasing your question might include:

- Will I be successful if I . . . ?
- What will be the outcome of . . . ?
- What is the future of my relationship with . . . ?
- What is coming up in my love life?
- How will my career progress with . . . ?
- What do I most need to be aware of concerning my finances?

For a general reading you could ask the cards for their wisdom on what is most important for you to know at this time. The type of question you ask may also depend upon which type of card spread you decide to use.

About Card Spreads

A card spread is sometimes referred to as a card layout and simply means the order, pattern, and position in which you place the cards, with each position providing a different perspective through the given title. We have provided a few different spreads we created to use with this deck that work well for us, following in just a moment. However, feel free to be creative and design your own spread; just decide what information you feel would be helpful and title each position accordingly. Then experiment until you find a format you're happy with. Some readers prefer to read in a simple line with no position title at all, determining beforehand how many cards they will draw.

The first thing to decide is which spread seems most appropriate for the situation, what you wish to know, and then which you prefer using. Most readers have a few favorite spreads; again it's all down to preference and what you feel works best for you. For instance, you can just as easily use the Summary Spread as the Relationship Spread regarding a question concerning a relationship; the positions just provide different perspectives.

Remember that the cards are referring to a future event, so if the response doesn't appear to make sense, allow some time for things to unfurl. It's a natural tendency for our rational mind to try to base the future on what we're already aware of, and the future often brings unknown factors into play.

To discover which spreads perform best for you, it can be insightful to keep a record of the card responses, such as: the date, question asked, spread used, the named cards that appeared in each position, and your prediction; then review it at a later date. Experience is an excellent teacher in helping fine-tune your future readings.

The Art of Reading

Reading the cards is rather like reading a good book. When you're thoroughly engrossed in a novel you're carried along by the story and, at some critical point, you turn the page over in anticipation for what follows. The result may leave you feeling satisfied (the story went the way you were hoping), disappointed (the author killed off your favorite character), surprised (an unexpected plot twist), or indifferent.

Imagine your cards in the same way as pages in a book, you read them in order, and as you turn them over you experience an emotional response to what you find. Sometimes we can get so caught up in the logical mind, thinking about what a card means or how it fits in relation to others, that we can miss what our subconscious already knows (that efficient PA again!). Once you turn the cards over, how do you feel — good, bad, surprised, or indifferent? Try to gauge your automatic emotional response.

Further clues are offered as to how the story fits together: it may flow easily, appear disjointed and disconnected, or start off heading in one direction, only to have a sudden twist at the end. The flow of the reading can reflect how you, or the seeker, will literally experience forthcoming events. All these little clues are present before starting to analyze the meanings. (Sounds like an Agatha Christie!) This is particularly relevant in the Story Spread style of reading, covered shortly.

Open Book Spread

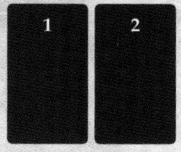

The Open Book Spread can be useful when you want a quick or insightful response to a particular query; it was inspired by Bibliomancy, as mentioned in the Introduction, where a chosen book is opened randomly and a line or passage selected with closed eyes.

Some readers like to draw a daily card to meditate upon or to look at the influences for the day ahead. Whilst you could still do this, the Fortune Cards are designed with quite concise meanings, so they tend to work better when read in combination with other cards. Using two cards can be helpful in becoming familiar and practiced in developing "the story," as you see how the cards relate and read from one to the next. If you decide to use this spread on a daily basis, then just be aware that the context of the meaning will probably be in a lesser capacity, more in alignment with daily happenings rather than a monthly reading, for instance.

Whichever method you decide to employ with this spread, simply shuffle and cut in your usual way and draw the first two cards from the top of the deck. The cards are read together from left to right, and the first situation leads into the second, similar to The Story Spread.

Summary Spread

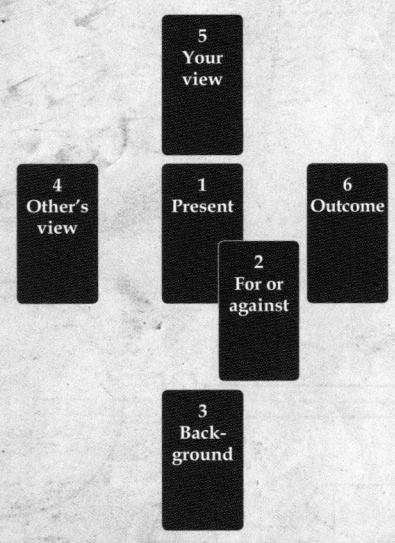

The Summary Spread is useful for answering a specific question. Shuffle and cut in the usual way whilst asking your question and place the cards as shown.

Card 1: Indicates the present situation, or what is being experienced.
Card 2: Represents what is working for or against the situation.
Card 3: Provides the history or background in relation to the question.
Card 4: How other people view the matter or a specific person if they were named in the question.
Card 5: How you view the situation—your thoughts and feelings about it.
Card 6: The potential outcome.

Alternate Realities Spread

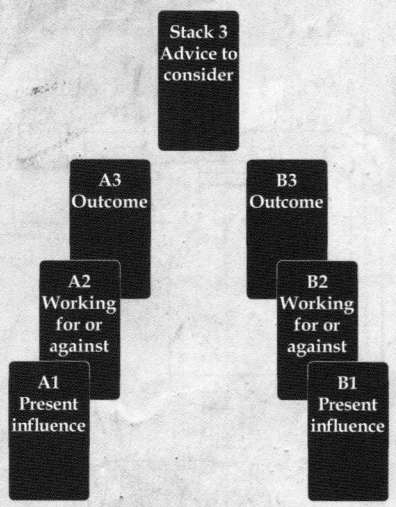

A useful spread when there is the choice of two options; just focus your intention on what option A and B represent in the question.

For instance: Option A: accepting a new job offer. Option B: stay with existing company. This provides the opportunity to compare the potential future of each option. The second card in each area can be quite revealing.

1) Shuffle and cut the cards into three in the usual way, but don't regather them.
2) Take the first stack dropped and deal the cards from the top to the left side, as in the spread. This side represents Option A.
3) Take the second stack dropped and deal the cards from the top to the right side, as shown. This side represents Option B.
4) Take the third stack and place the top card as shown. This card provides overall advice to consider.

Relationship Spread

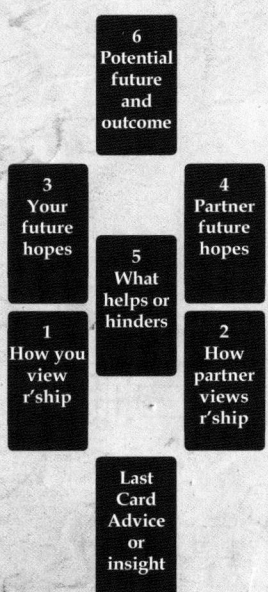

Concentrate on the relationship in question whilst shuffling. (This can be any type of relationship, not just romantic.) Cut into three and stack in the usual way.

Card 1: How you view the relationship.
Card 2: How the named person views the relationship.
Card 3: Your hopes for the future of the relationship.
Card 4: What the named person hopes for the future of the relationship.
Card 5: What helps or hinders this relationship.
Card 6: The potential future or outcome of this relationship.
Card 7: The very last card, at the bottom of the deck, is advice or hidden insight.

Sequel Spread

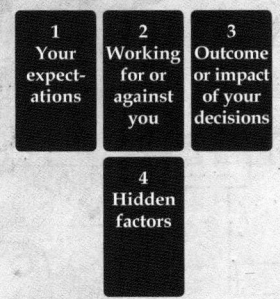

The Sequel Spread shows the subsequent course of events, or the impact of a decision that you're contemplating.

Formulate the question, such as: What would be the outcome if I . . . ? or What impact would my decision to . . . have on my . . . (finances, job, family, etc.).

Shuffle and cut the deck into three, but don't regather them.

1) The top card from the first stack shows your expectations.
2) The top card from the second stack shows what is or will be working for or against you.
3) The top card taken from the third stack shows what the impact or outcome will be.
4) Turn the third stack over and take the bottom card; this reveals other hidden factors you should be aware of.

Story Spread

The Story Spread uses a slightly different approach as we read three cards together in a line to create a flowing narrative. As we mentioned within some of the card definitions, this is when a card preceding or following will be particularly relevant.

The first card drawn indicates the theme or subject, or "what it's all about." Think of it like the book cover that provides a flavor of what's inside.

The three cards underneath supply insight as to how the situation will progress. Consider these like the pages of the book: we read them in order from left to right and each one provides more information, moving forward in time as the story and action progresses. You can address a specific question, or ask the cards what you most need to be aware of as a general question.

Create Your Theme

An alternative way of working with this spread is to take a card from the deck to place in the Theme position, to focus your intention to represent one particular aspect of your life that you would like to know about. (In other traditions, such as Tarot and Lenormand, this is known as the Significator card.) You then shuffle the rest of the deck whilst asking your question, cut in the usual way and place the three cards below, as shown.

For example, if your question concerned finance, you could use Treasure as your Theme card, Castle for home or property, Guardian of the Books for work, etc. The main consideration with this method is that if you remove a card from the deck, then you're taking it out of play, so it can't appear in the reading. For instance, if a single lady wanted to know if there was a new relationship on the horizon, then we would leave Kissed in the deck, because it is one of the cards we would look for, and so use The Heroine for the Theme card instead.

If you prefer using a Theme card, but wish to leave the main indicator cards in the deck, you can use the seeker's card to represent yourself, i.e., The Hero for a male seeker, or The Heroine for female.

Story Spread Reading Technique

If you've ever had the joy of listening to a very young child telling a story, you may have noticed that the story usually forges ahead omitting any pauses, with lots of "and then" replacing full stops. When they first start to write their stories, this is often the case too, before they fully understand or master punctuation. This is a good example of how the three cards link together. Just imagine "and then" inserted in between each one, or "this leads to."

If you're familiar with Josie's *Easy Tarot* books, this is a similar reading style, where each card or situation leads into the next one. For Lenormand users you'll find it's a slightly different technique, although the cards offer a good degree of flexibility if you choose to use them in a different way.

The Story Spread works slightly differently from the previous spreads shown, where each card is read in relationship to the title of the position with a clear structure. With the Story Spread you are working with a series of events, each following one another, and the order in which the card appears represents the order in which they will arrive. If you find yourself racing ahead and the following cards distract you, try placing them face down first, and then turn them over as you read each one in order. As you become more adventurous you may also decide to use more than three cards.

Whichever spreads you decide to use allow some time for the results to unfold. If you repeatedly ask questions concerning the same issues in a short period of time, the cards' response could become jumbled or contradictory.

In the following examples we have provided two readings that we conducted for different people, to show how the approaches can differ when applied.

Example Story Spread With Theme Card

For this reading, we took Treasure out of the deck first, to use as the Theme card. The seeker then shuffled the deck whilst asking what was going to happen concerning their finances. The three cards drawn were The Songbird, Downfall, and The Gatekeeper.

Using just the keywords we can see: feeling restricted by the situation (this leads to) Downfall, a card of defeat, feeling spent and efforts not realized (and then) The Gatekeeper unlocks the problem and provides a lucky escape from the situation.

If the order had appeared as: The Songbird, The Gatekeeper, Downfall then it would show something releasing them from the restriction, but then heading towards the defeat of the Downfall card. Although the original reading shows that the Downfall card may still be experienced, it eventually leads to a positive outcome.

Example Story Spread Without Theme Card

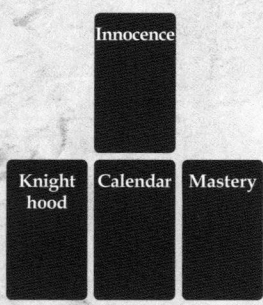

In this reading, the seeker asked what they most needed to be aware of at this time. A Theme card was not chosen from the deck. Innocence, Knighthood, Calendar, and Mastery were pulled.

Innocence as the main theme informs us that the reading concerns a child. Knighthood reveals they will receive an award or honor, leading to something being built steadily before achieving Mastery. Given the placement of the Knighthood card we can see this should happen quite soon.

If the order of the cards had appeared as Calendar, Knighthood, Mastery, then it could imply quite some time (months or years) before the award or honor is achieved, although once it is, then Mastery follows soon after. So the position in which the cards appear and the order in which you read them makes a difference in the interpretation of how events will unfold.

Indications for Time

Generally, we find that the results from readings can take up to a maximum of a year, at most, but three to six months is a fairly good average. Some events may start to happen quite quickly, whilst others can take longer.

Some of the cards naturally reflect speed and movement, such as Pegasus and Time Flies, whilst Calendar or Lady Winter have a much slower energy, so their appearance can be useful indicators when gauging the speed of events.

Providing specific timing is quite tricky, since the nature of events in our lives is not cast in stone and there are many variables that can affect how soon things come to pass. Overall, we feel it's always best to consider time loosely, as an approximation rather than a fixed date.

Lady Spring, Lady Summer, Lady Autumn, and Lady Winter, all carry months of the year relevant to the season they represent and so they can be used to indicate a particular time period of three months. If any of these cards appear in your spread then please read the definition first as part of your reading, then the time period shown as a secondary factor.

Guidelines for timing with the Season cards:

- The Season cards do not count towards timing if they appear in a past or present position. For instance, in the Summary Spread, positions 1 and 3 would not count.
- Use the first Season card that appears in the relevant positions, if there is more than one in the spread.

If you wish, you can take this a step further to calculate an approximate week, by using the number on a card.

There are two factors to remember for this method:

- All the numbers after card number 13 are reduced to a single digit by adding the two numbers together, so number 14 would be 5 (1 + 4 = 5). Always reduce a number that totals more than thirteen because 13 x 4 = 52 weeks in the year.
- Take the final card in the spread as the number you need, unless it is the Season card being used; in that instance, go backwards for the next number, as the Season card can't represent both the month and number of weeks.

Take the first Season card that appears in a relevant position, then the number from the final card, to represent the number of weeks from the beginning of the time period of the Season card.

Example to calculate time period:

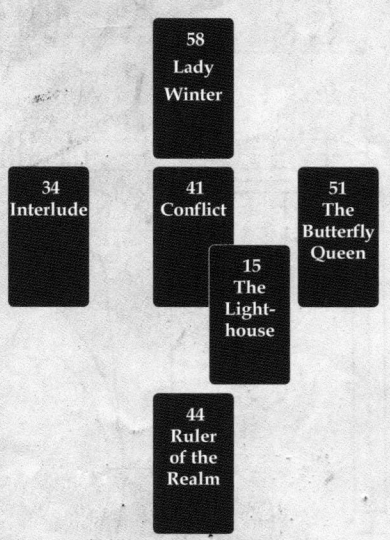

Lady Winter falls in a relevant position to use as the Season card.

The final card is The Butterfly Queen, numbered 51. As this is more than thirteen we add the two digits together, $5 + 1 = 6$.

The approximate timing shown calculates as 6 weeks from the beginning of December.

Reading for Others

Most people use their cards for self-readings and personal guidance, but there may come a point when you feel ready to read the cards for others. As you've probably noticed, there's an intentional parallel with cartomancy in the story from the Mastery card. When someone consults the cards, they are seeking their own Book of Destiny, the answers to questions concerning their future, and you then become the Guardian of the Books, imparting the wisdom of the cards in order to help them.

If this is your first introduction to card divination, then you may be surprised to learn that there are many thousands of people around the world involved in the art of cartomancy from various traditions. Whether they practice professionally or as a pastime, most readers follow a code of ethics to uphold and promote responsible use, and for the benefit of those who place trust in them as a reader. Most cartomancers have great respect for their cards and the caring service they provide, so if you decide to join their ranks you become a reflection of their tradition. If someone behaves badly, it can create the wrong impression and damage the reputation of those associated with card reading.

Reading for others can be an enjoyable and rewarding experience but it also carries a level of trust and responsibility, so we have provided a few basic guidelines to consider concerning ethics below.

Ethics and Responsible Reading

- The seeker will most likely impart personal information during their reading, so always honor their trust with your confidentiality.
- If you receive questions concerning legal, financial, or health matters,

you need to be careful that you're not providing specific advice if you're not qualified as a professional to do so, otherwise you may fall foul of the law. Should any of these areas raise concern in the reading, then it's best to advise the seeker to consult a registered specialist.
- Some readers will not read for minors at all, whilst others may only do so if they have parental consent. Young people can be impressionable, so exercise care.
- You should only read for the seeker present, so if the question involves another person, then it should be phrased in a way that directly relates to the seeker; this could otherwise be considered as third-party reading, or snooping.
- Approach your readings with sensitivity and respect from a place of non-judgment, with the aim to help the seeker maintain control of their own life. Our goal is to assist and empower the seeker through reading what we see in the cards, to help them consider or explore their options.

Clearing the Cards

After finishing a reading, shuffle and cut the cards before placing them back into your chosen container ready for next time. When the cards have been used to do a reading for someone else, then we like to completely separate the deck by dealing the cards from the top into six piles, then collect the piles back up in an alternate order (1-3-5-2-4-6) and shuffle well. This is just a practical way to be certain they're fully separated before next use.

Some readers like to periodically cleanse their cards by passing them through the smoke of sage incense or storing them with a natural crystal. If we ever sense the cards just don't feel right, or if a reading hasn't been very positive, we tend to separate and shuffle thoroughly and sometimes sleep with them under the pillow again. You can also place them on an inside window ledge in the moonlight.

Whatever method you decide to use is mainly down to your own beliefs and preferences.

How Accurate are the Readings?

It's generally considered that no method of prediction is one hundred per cent accurate. There are some life events that may be unavoidable, but to a large extent people do have some control over their lives through free will, choice, and then the actions they take in the circumstances presented to them.

Our actions and interactions with others create forward momentum that set events into motion, so the reading will usually reflect the probable future and outcome of that path. The cards can be excellent in highlighting unexpected events that may arise on the way. Most future events are not set in stone or predetermined, so the cards provide good guidance for the seeker to consider their options.

Epilogue

Having lived within the world of *The Chronicles of Destiny* for more than two years, we admit to feeling somewhat reluctant to emerge from this magical realm. Yet as the story from the Alchemy card reminds us, we can enter the Kingdom whenever we choose. The Butterfly Queen is calling to whisk everything away to the publisher as the set enters the next stage on its journey to reach you.

We hope you have enjoyed our time together and that the characters will hold a special place in your everyday world as they do in ours, and that this book and cards are helpful in guiding your course. If you're a Weaver of Words, then we also hope you find the deck useful for inspiration, brainstorming ideas, and developing plots, as you write and create your stories.

We wish you a successful quest of exploration and discovery filled with many happy and magical adventures!

For the moment, our time has come to a close, but please share your stories and experiences of the book and deck with us at the website: **www.thechroniclesofdestiny.com**.

For now, if you'll kindly excuse us, there is a book beckoning, gently whispering our name...

Josie & Emily

Keywords at a Glance

The following table provides all the keywords for the cards, like a "cheat sheet," for quick and easy access. Please see the relevant chapters for full interpretations.

Chapter	Title	Keywords
1	The Enchanted Emporium	Learning and study. Refining skills. Apprentice. Curiosity provides opportunity for discovery. A path that leads to greater awareness.
2	Guardian of the Books	Occupation or workplace. Dedication to work.
3	The Hero	Male seeker. Female seeker's partner.
4	The Heroine	Female seeker. Male seeker's partner.
5	Dreams	Future plans, goals, and dreams, but a need to take action to make them a reality. Aspirations and ambitions. Negative aspect: wishful thinking or being unrealistic.
6	The Call	An offer being made to you; a proposal or invitation that prompts a call to action.

Chapter	Title	Keywords
7	Whispering Hall	Self-doubt, insecurity, lack of confidence. Ignoring problems or denial.
8	The Elder	Elderly relatives or a person of mature years. Taking advice from people with more life experience. Maturity and wisdom.
9	Accepting the Quest	Contracts, agreements, transactions. Making a formal commitment. Pledging your oath. Taking up the challenge.
10	The Adventure	All types of new beginnings, the start of something new, taking a new path in life.
11	Innocence	Children or birth. Embracing life with a sense of wonder. Keeping an open heart and mind. Playfulness, joy, and innocence.
12	The Lightbearer	Someone showing kindness to you. Gifts, generosity, and favors.
13	Time Flies	Time flies. Fast moving timeframe; things happening quickly.
14	Distant Shores	Foreign connection, people, or places. International trade. A long journey. Expanding your horizons to move outside your comfort zone. Unfamiliar places.

Chapter	Title	Keywords
15	The Lighthouse	Warning sign, a red flag. Something demands your attention. Danger; proceed with caution.
16	Sinking Ship	Loss of all kinds but particularly financial loss or difficulty. Failed plans.
17	Shore of Trials	Challenging times. Trials and tribulations. Difficulty, upheavals, stress, (may show strained relationships).
18	Road to Nowhere	Dead end or full stop. Reconsider plans, a new route is needed.
19	Pegasus	Short journey. Flying visit. Forward momentum, going places. Speed, gets things moving. Transport.
20	The Warlock	Delays and hold-ups. Obstacles. Sometimes theft.
21	The Baroness	Underhandedness. Deceit. Hidden enemy. False friends or someone not working in your favor. Manipulation. Jealousy and gossip, someone with a poisonous tongue.
22	Masquerade	Illusionary situations. Everything may not be as it seems, be careful who you trust. Secrecy. Confusion and clouded thinking.

Chapter	Title	Keywords
23	The Songbird	Restriction, feeling caged in, stuck, or trapped. Dissatisfied with circumstances. Self-inflicted bad habits, addictions, unhealthy relationship.
24	The Dragon	Worries or anxiety. Fears, real or imagined, are preventing you from moving forward.
25	Downfall	Defeat and resignation, feeling spent. Efforts not realized. Letting go.
26	Sorrow	Sadness and regret. One-sided efforts. Unrequited love.
27	Word on Wing	Messages and news coming in through any form of communication.
28	Forest Labyrinth	Making a choice. Considering options, a decision is required.
29	The Gatekeeper	Unlocks obstacles or secrets; doors being opened for you. A lucky escape.
30	Balance	Balancing different aspects of a situation or keeping a balance in life. Finding equilibrium. Mental and emotional stability found through balance.

Chapter	Title	Keywords
31	The Dreamcatcher	Protection from bad influences. Ability to land on your feet. Synchronicity at work behind the scenes.
32	Waterfall	Health and well-being, vitality, healing. Going with the flow and trusting the process. Patience.
33	The Fellowship	Friendship and loyalty, reliable and steadfast. Helpful friends and allies lending support. Teamwork.
34	Interlude	Pause, rest, pulling resources together. Fact gathering. Taking time out.
35	Shooting Star	Good omens. Good luck and good fortune. Bright prospects. Persevere in your goals. Believe in yourself.
36	Kissed	Love and romance. Falling in love. Deep affection and heart-felt emotions.
37	Polaris	Something important becoming known to you that provides direction and guidance. A moment of inspiration.
38	Weaver of Words	Small ideas with big potential, ideas taking off and taking form. The power of words; tact and diplomacy. Writers.

Chapter	Title	Keywords
39	Resolve	Resolve. Determination. Taking action. Having the courage of your convictions.
40	Phoenix	Rebirth, second chances, revival, reinvention, something resurrected.
41	Conflict	Conflicts. Arguments, quarrels, strife, and upheavals.
42	Victory	Victory. Triumph. Success. Achievement. You will come up trumps.
43	Book of Destiny	Destiny is created when you actively pursue it. Whilst fate may present certain circumstances, destiny unfolds once you move towards it. Action shapes destiny.
44	Ruler of the Realm	Higher powers of authority, the law, officials, large institutions and structured organizations.
45	Knighthood	Awards and honors, promotion, recognition, approval from others. Someone holds you in high esteem or thinks highly of you.
46	Treasure	Money and material possessions, usually improvement. Finance. Someone or something precious to you; valued and treasured.
47	Union	Commitment. Marriage celebrations. Permanency. Settled, happy relationship.

Chapter	Title	Keywords
48	Bliss	Happiness and contentment. Celebrations, a time of joy.
49	Calendar	Slow timeframe, months or years. Slow movement but steady progress and lasting. Delay or longevity, depending upon placement.
50	Alchemy	Something ordinary has the potential to turn into something extraordinary. You only get out of something what you put into it, but you have the ingredients to create something special.
51	The Butterfly Queen	Catalyst for change; brings a major transition and transformation. Metamorphosis. The winds of change.
52	Castle	Your home is your castle. Home and family. Property. Stability.
53	Review	Reviewing, taking stock, answers lie in the past and past actions, reflection. Past experiences. Memories.
54	Mastery	Mastery. Integrating what you have learnt by applying skills and talents. Graduation.
SC. 55	Lady Spring	Green shoots, growth, new life, fertility (possible pregnancy with Innocence). A new cycle beginning. Renewal. Timing card: March, April, May.

Chapter	Title	Keywords
SC. 56	Lady Summer	Blossoming, in its prime, cause for celebration, hive of activity. Timing card: June, July, August.
SC. 57	Lady Autumn	Abundance, harvest, fruitful endeavors, collecting rewards, matters bearing fruit (with Innocence may represent a birth). Timing card: September, October, November.
SC. 58	Lady Winter	Frozen. Patience required, matters developing although they can't be seen. Quiet and solitude, dormant period, withdrawal, feeling isolated, an indifferent heart. Timing card: December, January, February.
SC. 59	Hero II	Can be used as an alternative card to switch with The Heroine for same sex reading, or an extra card to include where another man may feature in a question. A mystery man, "tall, dark stranger," another potential love interest or rival.
SC. 60	Heroine II	Can be used as an alternative card to switch with The Hero for same sex reading, or an extra card to include where another woman may feature in a question. A mystery woman, "beautiful stranger," another potential love interest or rival.

Bibliography

Campbell, Joseph. *The Hero With a Thousand Faces*. (London: Paladin Books, 1988).

Cheung, Theresa. *The Dream Dictionary From A to Z*. (London: HarperElement, 2006).

Coke, Edward. The Third Part of the Institutes of the Laws of England (1628); ch. 73, p. 162, quoted in Angela Partington, ed. *Oxford Dictionary of Quotations*. (Oxford, England: Oxford University Press, 1993, p. 209).

Crisp, Tony. *Dream Dictionary, An A to Z Guide to Understanding Your Unconscious Mind*. (New York, NY: Dell Publishing, 2002).

Ellershaw, Josephine, and Ciro Marchetti. *Easy Tarot: Learn to Read the Cards Once and For All!* (Woodbury, MN: Llewellyn Publications, 2007).

Matthews, John and Caitlin. *The Element Encyclopedia of Magical Creatures*. (London: HarperElement, 2005).

Vogler, Christopher. *The Writer's Journey: Mythic Structure for Writers*, Third Edition. (Chelsea, MI: Sheridan Books, Inc., 2007).

"The Four Seasons: The Living Countryside." (London: Reader's Digest, 1990).

About the Authors

Josephine Ellershaw

Josephine Ellershaw's experience with cartomancy began from an early age and now spans four decades. She has many years of professional experience providing Tarot readings, personal development, mentoring, and guidance to an International clientele. She is the author of bestseller, *Easy Tarot: Learn to Read the Cards Once and For All* and *Easy Tarot Reading: The Process Revealed in Ten True Readings*. Josie lives in North Yorkshire, England.

Emily Ellershaw

Emily Ellershaw grew up surrounded by books and Tarot cards, which influenced her passion for writing and cartomancy. She is an English Literature graduate and lives with her husband in North Yorkshire, England, where she now has her own ever-expanding library and card collection.

Josie and Emily always appreciate hearing from their readers, so please visit their website:

www.thechroniclesofdestiny.com

About the Artist

Claudia McKinney

Claudia McKinney is a professional digital artist specializing in book covers for bestselling authors, such as Amanda Hocking and Kami Garcia. Claudia is mom to four wonderful children and wife to Michael McKinney, residing in the beautiful seaside community of Carlsbad, California. Please visit her website:

www.phatpuppyart.com

Notes:

Notes:

Notes:

Notes:

Notes:

Notes: